Praise for *Side by Side Leadership* WITHDRAWN

"Dennis Romig has a real feel for the difficulties managers and leaders face in today's tough environment. *Side by Side Leadership* provides some great ideas on how to best utilize our most valuable resource, our people. It can be a critical part of the development and education of our new generation of leaders."

Jim Doran
Vice President, Manufacturing and Technology
Advanced Micro Devices

"I've seen the 300 percent improvements in business results first hand! There's no exaggeration here. If truly embraced, the model and tools will unlock the power of an organization or work group to surpass expectations."

G. C. "Chip" Gill
Vice President, Membership and Strategic Planning
Independent Petroleum Association of America

"If you want to fully engage your organization to achieve dramatic results, read and study *Side by Side Leadership*. Its easy-to-read, logical and simple concepts will move your organization to a much higher level of performance."

Charles D. Davidson
President & CEO, Noble Affiliates
Former Chairman, President & CEO, Vastar Resources, Inc.

"This book can save organizations millions of dollars associated with lost productivity and turnover. *Side by Side Leadership*'s emphasis on the 'whole person at work' can help to release previously untapped human potential and will enhance the longevity (retention) of the organization's most valuable assets — its trained and experienced people."

Barbara J. Kreisman
Sr. Consultant, Executive & Organization Development
Dell Computer Corporation

"A fantastic job of distilling the wisdom of thousands of research studies into a practical digest of useful ideas, principles, and strategies. A valuable resource for any contemporary leader who wants to learn how to develop collaborative leadership skills."

Steven A. Beebe, Ph.D.
Professor and Chair, Department of Speech Communication
Associate Dean, College of Fine Arts and Communication
Southwest Texas State University

"The same people that benefited from *The 7 Habits of Highly Effective People* will gain a great deal, both professionally and personally, from *Side by Side Leadership*."

Nancy Powell Bartlett
Performance Consultant
City of Irving, Texas

"This new model of leadership will show you how to understand and be successful in the new global economy. It's a great resource for people who are already managers and those who aspire to management positions."

Terry Ross
Vice President, Product Marketing
Primus Knowledge Solutions

"A dynamic and challenging book that overturns the view that classical top-down leadership or 'mandated empowerment' achieves effective performance. *Side by Side Leadership* provides a blueprint to develop partnerships which result in both organization and individual success."

Les Bowd
Director, Executive Development
Faculty of Management, University of Calgary

"Thought-provoking, 'on-the-job tested' information that encourages people to think differently about the process of leading others. Strong introduction to 'systems thinking' with new approaches to old problems."

Daniel V. Papero, Ph.D.
Director, The Bowen Center for the Study of the Family and
Crossway Community

"Lays out a roadmap of becoming a more balanced and effective leader. Training and development professionals, performance coaches, managers, executives, HR directors, and entrepreneurs — all who want to increase their value will find *Side by Side Leadership* a practical and important asset."

Mike Bown
Training & Development Manager
International SEMATECH

"Full of inspiring ideas and practical tips. *Side by Side* will help anyone rethink his organization from top to bottom."

Robert Klitgaard, Ph.D.
Dean, RAND Graduate School

"Very stimulating! The stories about others helped me visualize my actions, and the book gave me more 'tools' to use in my own leadership development. Will benefit leaders at all levels of the organization."

Charles Davenport
Manager, Motorola

"*Side by Side Leadership* unlocks the flow of talent and productivity. Dennis Romig uses solid data and current multifaceted research to transform 'soft' leadership skills into no-nonsense formulas."

Bev Powell
Manager, Tech Transfer and Performance Solutions
Intel Corporation

"A very strong presentation of the skills needed to achieve better morale, higher performance, and more effective leadership. Highly recommended for any current and aspiring leader in any organization."

Bob Watt
President & CEO
Seattle Chamber of Commerce

"*Side by Side Leadership* was used constantly to have the newly completed Houston Astros' Enron Field be the one publicly funded sports stadium to be completed on time and on budget."

Jim Jard
Board Member
Houston Sports Authority

"Allows people to comprehend and develop for themselves a dynamic, logical, adaptable model for effective leadership."

Matt Rollins
Training Coordinator, Advanced Micro Devices

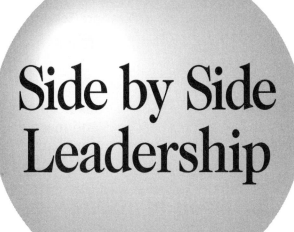

Side by Side Leadership

*Achieving
Outstanding Results
Together*

Dennis A. Romig, Ph.D.

Austin • Atlanta

Side by Side Leadership
Achieving Outstanding Results Together

Bard Press
An imprint of Longstreet Press
2140 Newmarket Parkway, Suite 122
Marietta, GA 30067
770-980-1488 voice, 770-859-9894 fax
www.bardpress.com

Side by Side Leadership® and Side by Side® are registered trademarks of Performance Resources, Inc.

Ordering Information
To order additional copies, contact your local bookstore or call 800-204-3118. Quantity discounts are available.

ISBN 1-885167-51-2 hardcover

Library of Congress Cataloging-in-Publication Data

Romig, Dennis A.
 Side by side leadership : achieving outstanding results together / Dennis A. Romig
  p. cm.
 Includes bibliographical references and index.
 ISBN 1-885167-51-2
  1. Leadership. 2. Teams in the workplace. I. Title.

HD57.7 .R65 2001
658.4'092--dc21   2001037687

The author may be contacted at the following address:
Dennis A. Romig
dromig@sidebyside.com

Credits
Editor: Jeff Morris
Proofreaders: Deborah Costenbader, Luke Torn
Index: Linda Webster
Cover design: Hespenheide Design
Text design/production: Jeff Morris

First printing: August 2001

Contents

Let me introduce myself. . . .

My name is Dennis Romig, and I will be your Side by Side Leadership coach. My colleagues and I have discovered a new way to coach leaders to improve business results fast — so fast and so well that even I was a little surprised. One company, which you will read about in this book, realized a gain of several billion dollars!

One thing that surprised me was that Side by Side Leadership works anywhere. Training and coaching developed for high-tech companies (Texas Instruments, Advanced Micro Devices, Dell Computer) brought outstanding results in other organizations as well — energy companies, agriculture, retail, real estate, manufacturing, health care, government, even religious organizations.

To understand how Side by Side Leadership came to be, it would help you to know something about my background. In high school and college, I was avidly interested in science and studied biology and chemistry. I later completed a doctoral degree in educational psychology and management at the University of Texas. During my studies, I asked my professors, "Where is the scientific proof for all these psychology and management theories?" The answer was often, "There isn't any."

However, I felt sure that high-quality research might answer my questions about how leaders influence organizational productivity. This book is based on my reviews of 3,000 studies of leadership and management, as well as studies in biology, neurophysiology, and Murray Bowen's Natural Systems Theory.

I am now president of Performance Resources, Inc., in Austin, Texas, working with a group of talented people. We call ourselves a "think and do tank." The "think" part is the research we collect and analyze; the "do" is the practical skills in our training materials and consulting. The successes (and failures) of the "do" feed back into improving the "think."

I wrote this book to make Side by Side Leadership available for you and others. Give it a try. Let me know how it goes.

Part

I

The New
Leadership Model

The world of business has changed radically over the last several decades. It's gone global, and it's become a whole lot more competitive. But in this rapidly evolving business climate, one thing hasn't kept pace: leadership. Top-down leadership is still the usual approach, even though it is minimally effective. Part I presents a new model of leadership that promotes improvements in team and organizational performance of 25 percent or more — actual results, as supported by research and field experience.

Chapter 1

Muddle in the Middle

The Current State of Leadership, Its Effect on Productivity, and the Promise of a Third Way of Leading

You and I are alone in the conference room. I am sitting at the table with your company's materials and reports spread in front of me. You are pacing back and forth, hands waving, talking excitedly.

"The problem is, we're only increasing our performance by 4 or 5 percent a year!" You pick up a marker and draw a nearly horizontal line on the whiteboard:

US ⎯⎯⎯⎯⎯⎯⎯⎯⎯ 4%

"That's not good enough. Our competitors' productivity is way up here." You draw another line above the first:

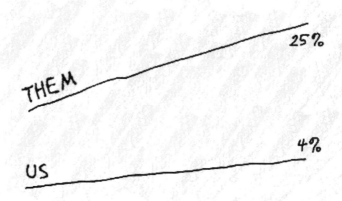

"We're getting left behind! We've got to grow, we've got to get a lot more productive. We need big step increases." You draw a stepped line on the board between your current performance and your desired improvement:

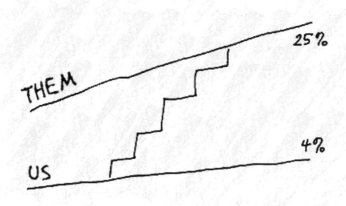

"This is what we need," you say, jabbing at the third line. "We have to improve our performance by 20 or 30 percent a year to overtake them."

You've called me in to consult because you've heard about Performance Resources, Inc., and the performance improvements it has helped other companies achieve. I've had much the same conversation with executives, managers, supervisors, and team leaders in a wide range of organizations: high-techs, like Advanced Micro Devices, Dell Computer, Motorola, and Texas Instruments; manufacturers such as Asea Brown Boveri, Dow Corning, Monsanto, and Westinghouse; natural resource companies including Amoco, Arco, and Vastar Resources; even local, state, and federal governments.

"I've been told that other organizations have realized productivity and performance gains of anywhere from 30 to 300 percent," you say. "Tell me what we have to do to get that kind of improvement."

"First, I'd like to ask you something," I reply. "How good a job are your leaders doing? Are they effective? Do your employees work well with them?"

"I hear a lot of employee complaints about some of our managers," you reply. "Nobody likes working for them. We move the managers to new positions, and the people there start complaining. Either the subordinates transfer into another division, or they stay where they are and not much work gets done."

"How many of your supervisors and managers are running into this kind of trouble?"

"I'd say at least half of them don't know quite how to treat their subordinates, or even their peers. You know, it's funny, but these are good people. It's just that when you put them in positions of responsibility, in charge of others, their worst impulses come out. They become demanding, autocratic. Some of them turn into tyrants."

"So you'd say that the common denominator is that these good people that you put in charge of teams and operations feel compelled to exercise more authority? They try to be the 'boss'?"

"Yes, that's right. Even though that's not our intention, that seems to be what happens. We promote them, we set goals for their new teams, and we let them handle things as they see fit. They start giving orders, and first thing you know everybody's complaining and resisting. The result is that they rarely meet their goals or deadlines."

A Familiar Pattern

"Okay," I say. "What you're describing is the 'top-down' leadership style. The ideas and the orders come from the top. They're handed down to subordinates without discussion, and subordinates are expected to follow them without objection. Does that sound familiar?"

"Yes. Exactly."

"Unfortunately," I say, "top-down doesn't work well in business anymore. The work force is better educated, and the business environment changes faster. To survive, you have to use your employees' knowledge and skills more effectively, and you have to give them the ability to respond to the changes. Top-down managers can't react fast enough.

"And top-down leadership is all too common. About half of all managers, supervisors, and executives fail to lead effectively because they make this basic mistake. I can show you plenty of hard research that supports this conclusion — research based on ratings by these leaders' subordinates, peers, and supervisors, and on objective assessments such as goal achievement.[1]

"Fifty percent failure! Just think of the productivity your organization could achieve if your leadership became 70, 80, or 90 percent effective!"

You agree. "I know we'd be in a lot better competitive shape now with better leadership."

Old Behaviors

"Now let's see what's going on in your company," I say. "Tell me what top-down leadership behaviors you see in the following leadership functions. Start with communication." As you describe your organization's traits, I take notes summarizing your comments.

> To survive, you have to use your employees' knowledge and skills more effectively and let them respond to changes.

LEADERSHIP FUNCTIONS	TOP-DOWN BEHAVIORS
Communication	Supervisors and managers do all the talking. Followers are supposed to listen and obey. Communication is one-way.
Decision making	Supervisors & managers make all the important decisions & force them on others.
Teamwork & helpfulness	Supervisors & managers demand help from everyone else & generally do not take time to help others.
Identifying causes of problems	Supervisors & managers see problems as someone else's fault rather than recognizing multiple contributing factors, including their own role in the problem.
Drawing on new resources to solve problems & achieve goals	Supervisors & managers talk with only a very narrow circle of colleagues.
Emotional balance & maturity	Supervisors & managers under pressure tend to either get angry with others or go off & sulk.

"What about employees' behavior?" I ask.

"The biggest problems are low performance and low productivity. People simply refuse to work well for the top-down bosses — especially the self-motivated, hard-working, smart people. The best workers leave."

Old Definitions of Leadership

"Let's talk about what we mean by leadership," I say. "How would you define leadership?"

You think for a minute. "I guess I think of it as the ability to get people to follow you and carry out your wishes. But I think I'll go with what my dictionary says." You find your *Webster's* on a nearby shelf. "Let's see — here it is: 'the ability to direct, command, or guide a group or activity.'"[2]

"Sounds pretty top-down, doesn't it?" I say. "Particularly the words 'direct' and 'command.' But that's typical. Let me read you some definitions I've found in other books. Here's one from *The Essence of Leadership,* by Edwin Locke: 'the process of inducing others to take action toward a common goal.'[3] And here's a definition in Bernard Bass's *Handbook of Leadership*: 'the process of influencing the activities of an organized group in its efforts toward goal setting and goal achievement.'[4] And there are five other passages in Bass's book that define the leader along the lines of 'one who influences followers.'

LEADER

⇓

FOLLOWERS OR SUBORDINATES

"As you can see, most authorities think of leadership in top-down terms — something that is done to someone else." I go to the whiteboard, pick up a marking pen, and start drawing. "The concept is that the influencing is all one-way, from the top to the bottom. It's no wonder newly promoted supervisors and leaders think they're supposed to lead this way. That's what they learned from watching *their* bosses."

"I have to confess," you say, "I never liked bosses who treated me top-down, so I can understand why employees would resent it. But I couldn't find any good alternatives.

"I actually tried a different leadership approach I'd been hearing about. For our annual planning and budgeting process, I asked supervisors and managers to submit plans and budgets for anything they wanted to do. It gave me a pretty good jolt. The new spending they wanted was so high it would have driven us into bankruptcy.

"I can't just strip my managers of their authority and let employees do their own thing, or even do the leading, can I?"

"No," I reply, "you can't. What you're talking about is called 'bottom-up' leadership. Like this." I erase my arrow and redraw it pointing upward. "Some supervisors have gone to that extreme of participative management. Executives who spent their entire careers practicing autocratic leadership read Robert Greenleaf's *Servant Leadership* and did a complete turnaround.[5] But they misunderstood Greenleaf and others like him. They went too far. The proponents of participative management never meant to advocate a one-way, bottom-up model.

"Others have tried different approaches that fall somewhere between the extremes of top-down and bottom-up leadership. But like you, these other managers and supervisors have yet to find a way to lead that consistently increases productivity. There's still that muddle in the middle."

LEADER

↑

FOLLOWERS OR SUBORDINATES

"Well, neither top-down nor bottom-up has worked very well for us," you say. "I sometimes wonder if the term 'leadership' can even be used here."

"I used to find leadership just as confusing and confounding," I say. "The word had secrets I couldn't fathom, powers I couldn't unlock. I knew some leaders were great leaders, but I couldn't tell exactly why. It seemed like some kind of magic. I had no idea how to change my own leadership practices to get better results.

"But I decided I would discover those secrets, whatever it took. I set that as my goal. I began to dig and read. I searched through 3,000 leadership studies and books for an alternative to top-down and bottom-up leadership.

"And I found what I was looking for." I draw another figure on the board. "It sounds simple, but here's what I discovered: when leaders listen to contributors — and this is true both in teams and in the organization as a whole — when they share the leadership, productivity takes off.

"The kind of leadership I'm talking about is two-way, mutual, and interactive. This diagram shows a basic principle: the top arrow represents how the contributor talks first while the leader listens. The lower arrow is the leader presenting his or her ideas while the contributor listens. It's always a two-way interaction.

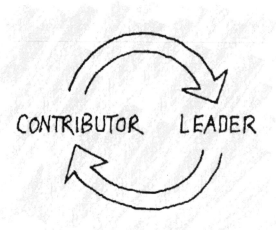

"This is basically what I'm going to show you over the next few days. I call this style of interaction 'Side by Side Leadership.' That's a term I settled on to distinguish it from both top-down and bottom-up leadership.

"You may have noticed I just used the word 'contributor' where you might have expected to hear 'follower.' I have a good reason for this. A follower can be anyone who passively follows orders. A follower does not have to think. A follower does not have to contribute ideas or share responsibility for success or failure.

"In Side by Side Leadership, I use the term 'contributor' to reflect the fact that many others besides the leader

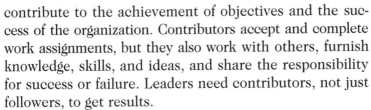

contribute to the achievement of objectives and the success of the organization. Contributors accept and complete work assignments, but they also work with others, furnish knowledge, skills, and ideas, and share the responsibility for success or failure. Leaders need contributors, not just followers, to get results.

"And in all that research I mentioned, the conclusions are clear: When leadership is shared and mutual, workers are more innovative. They get the work done faster and at less cost."

Side by Side Results

"I've come prepared for this meeting with you," I continue, "because I'm excited about what I've learned from the documented research I've found, along with my years of experience in the field." I briefly describe for you what I've learned in the course of my research:

- In companies where workers and leaders abandon old-style, top-down behavior and begin to share leadership, performance (productivity or profitability) improves by 15 percent within six months.

- When leaders lead their teams and work groups using Side by Side Leadership, quality, cost control, customer satisfaction, productivity, and profits rise by 20 to 40 percent within one year.

- Knowledge leaders — engineers, scientists, marketers, technicians, and other professionals — who develop and share their knowledge side by side are more productive than those who do not.[6]

- Organizations where most of the leaders use Side by Side Leadership techniques double or triple their organizational results within four years.

"My colleagues and I have also found that most leaders want their entire organization to improve together, not just particular teams or departments. For this to happen, Side by Side Leadership principles must be implemented in each of five spheres of influence — personal, interpersonal, team, organizational, and knowledge leadership." I reach into my briefcase and produce a sheet of paper with an unfamiliar graphic on it.

You ask me, "You mean I have to be a good leader in all five of these areas of leadership?"

"Fortunately for you, me, and everybody else in the world," I reply, "the answer is no. You don't have to be strong in all spheres at the same time. Very few people could ever hope to be. Most of us can be strong in one or two spheres at a time, but we are naturally weaker in others. But for the organization as a whole to improve and grow, it needs leadership in all five spheres."

Customized Leadership

"Let me give you an example. Here's the leadership profile of Hank, a first-line supervisor. Hank was a team leader we assessed for one of our clients. He was one of the highest-rated leaders in his organization. Notice that Hank's team leadership sphere is larger than his knowledge leadership sphere. Although his technical knowledge of the manufacturing equipment and methods was not high, Hank was a master of team facilitating. When he used the principles of Side by Side Leadership, his team's productivity went up 30 percent.

"This is only one of many potentially successful leadership patterns. No matter what your own interests and abilities, you can be a successful leader."

SIDE BY SIDE LEADERSHIP PRINCIPLES	HOW THE PRINCIPLES IMPROVE PERFORMANCE
1. Two-Way Street	Two-way communication, participation, and cooperation increase involvement and commitment.
2. Interaction Fields	Leaders create new resources by pulling in and creatively combining resources from outside interaction fields.
3. Visionary Goals	Shared visionary goals provide an elevating or transforming purpose for every interaction.
4. Focused Creativity	New ideas allow people to increase quality and productivity without working harder or longer.
5. Structured Participation	When every team and organization member participates in implementing decisions and setting goals, everyone works together to achieve the goals.
6. Proven Knowledge	Not all creative ideas and strategies can be implemented. Knowledge and experience can help select the best ideas for improving performance.
7. Transferred Authority	When workers have the authority to make the improvements they see in their work area without waiting for upper-management approval, the benefits are realized faster.

"That's interesting," you say. "How can I figure out my own profile?"

"There is a self-assessment you can use after you learn more about the five spheres of Side by Side Leadership influence," I reply.

"Well, when can I begin learning the basics?"

"I'll start you off right now," I say. "There are seven principles that will make up the foundation for everything you need to know. They're based on that research I told you about. Each principle is a part of the whole, a piece of the puzzle. Here's how each principle improves performance."

I begin describing the seven principles. As we discuss them, I jot down on the whiteboard a summary of the benefits of each principle.

"A leader who uses all seven of these principles, all seven pieces of the puzzle, *in each sphere of leadership influence* is more likely to achieve success." I draw a sphere on the whiteboard and divide it into seven puzzle pieces.

"Each of the five spheres can be thought of the same way — as an assemblage of seven parts. A leader can apply each of the seven principles when leading in any of the five spheres of influence. For example, developing shared visionary goals (Principle 3) in the team leadership sphere increases the likelihood of having a high-performance team with outstanding results.

"Another way to implement Side by Side Leadership is to learn and use a set of twenty skills." I hand you another printed page:

PERSONAL **LEADERSHIP**	Skill 1: Achieving Personal Visionary Goals Skill 2: Practicing Honesty and Fairness Skill 3: Maintaining Objectivity
KNOWLEDGE **LEADERSHIP**	Skill 4: Acquiring Knowledge Skill 5: Sharing Knowledge Skill 6: Transforming Knowledge
INTERPERSONAL **LEADERSHIP**	Skill 7: Two-Way Listening Skill 8: Mutual Contributing Skill 9: Connecting Visionary Goals Skill 10: Diverse Networking
TEAM **LEADERSHIP**	Skill 11: Managing the Interface Skill 12: Setting Team Goals Skill 13: Using Structured Team Skills Skill 14: Coordinating Team Roles Skill 15: Increasing Team Capacity
ORGANIZATIONAL **LEADERSHIP**	Skill 16: Identifying Opportunities and Threats Skill 17: Living Organizational Values Skill 18: Setting Organizational Visionary Goals Skill 19: Creating New Strategies Skill 20: Creating a Flexible Organization

"This shows how these twenty skills are related to the five spheres of leadership influence. But this doesn't mean each skill is limited to a particular sphere. Even though interpersonal listening, for example, is related to the interpersonal leadership sphere, a leader can also use that skill to succeed in the other spheres as well — personal, knowledge, team, and organizational leadership."

You look at my handouts, then at my scribblings on the whiteboard. You shake your head. "Pretty complicated. Seems a bit overwhelming."

"That's the bad news about Side by Side Leadership," I say. "It is a system model, and like all system models, it has many interrelated parts. It is complex, because leadership is not a simple thing. Never has been.

"But here's the good news: this system gives you many entry points. It gives you many ways to get started improving your own leadership, and the leadership of others, to increase productivity."

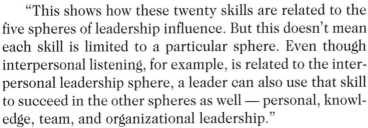

This system gives you many entry points — many ways to get started improving your own leadership and that of others.

You look doubtful. "I'm still not sure," you say.

"You sound like a colleague of mine named Ted. Let me tell you about him.

"Ted is a brilliant, creative executive, a very accomplished idea man, but not too long ago he found himself about to lose his job. He could come up with the most creative ideas for new business and marketing strategies, but nobody who worked for him would implement his ideas.

"We sat down with him and analyzed his leadership habits. Here's what we discovered.

"He often came into scheduled meetings, changed the agenda on the spot, and proceeded to talk about items of his own choosing. Unfortunately, the others in the meeting, unprepared for the topic, would often misunderstand or fail to follow his intentions.

"When he delegated work, he would later change what the person assigned to it had done. That person would quickly lose all enthusiasm for future tasks, and Ted would find it harder and harder to work with him.

"For efficiency, he limited his leadership interactions to just a few minutes of 'top-down' orders and instructions. But little got done, and the resistance and conflict that resulted would last for months. Whatever time Ted thought he was saving was quickly lost.

"We counseled Ted to give Side by Side Leadership a try. We guided him through the basics, through the five leadership spheres of influence, the seven principles, the twenty key skills. We showed him how to put them together, how to use them to set goals, solve problems, and accomplish objectives.

"Ted learned the value of a mutual sharing of information, knowledge, and experience when making a decision. He learned to slow down and listen, rather than simply issuing orders and turning to other matters. He learned to see his people as people, with ideas and skills and feelings and opinions, rather than as pieces to be moved around on a chessboard.

"Once he had grown accustomed to the principles and practices of two-way behaviors, Ted observed that applying Side by Side Leadership was like sailing with the wind at his back. He found that more work got done, with less emotional drag. He got along better with his contributors and co-workers. He found the experience exhilarating.

"Now I want to encourage you to try the principles, practices, and skills of Side by Side Leadership yourself. Watch how others respond. Measure the results you get in the first few months.

"And that," I say to you, "is basically what this book I'm giving you is all about. In the first few chapters you will find some practical tips that you can try out immediately to start improving your own performance and that of others.

"Using the principles of Side by Side Leadership presented in this book will transform your leadership abilities. It will raise your organization to new heights of efficiency, productivity, and profitability. Read it. Learn from it. Enjoy it. It will open your eyes."

The book is now in your hands.

Chapter 2

The Search for a Better Model

A Conceptual History of Leadership and the Quest for a More Productive Approach

You and I have heard and read much about the world's great leaders. We've long admired them. We've marveled at the success of their leadership:

Abraham Lincoln.

Alfred P. Sloan.

Mohandas Gandhi.

Martin Luther King Jr.

We've also known successful leaders in our own time, seen them in action in our own lives and professions — leaders who inspired us to greater effort and success. Like me, you've probably wondered: What made these people great leaders? Was it something they were born with? Was it the way they were raised or taught? Was it the times in which they lived, or perhaps the people or organizations they led? What was the critical difference?

As a businessman, I was also mystified. Some business leaders stood head and shoulders above others in terms of success. What, specifically, were the leadership skills and practices they used that improved performance, productivity, and profit? If these practices and skills could be isolated, they could be taught to others. It seemed to me that analyzing skills and practices would be far more helpful than simply compiling a list of great leaders' traits. As a professional who wanted to teach these skills and practices to others, I needed answers.

Researching the Literature

To find the answers, I set out to study whatever research had already been conducted. Most of what I wanted to know I found buried in journals in the dusty stacks of university libraries — journals of leadership research in business, management, psychology, economics, and other disciplines. In all, I reviewed almost 3,000 leadership studies.

After plowing through all these books and articles, however, I left these libraries feeling frustrated and discouraged. Most of the information was essentially useless. Few of the results were from field studies with control groups; most of the studies were based on questionnaires and surveys, anecdotal case histories, or responses from college students. Many of the conclusions were weak or contradictory. If current leadership books and training programs were based on research this bad, I thought, no wonder so many leaders failed.

> If current leadership books and training programs were based on research this bad, no wonder so many leaders failed.

I was after something more rigorous, more scientific. I wanted to identify research-based practices and skills that leaders could safely bet their careers on. So I narrowed my focus; I considered only field studies involving real leaders in real organizations, studies in which scientific measurements documented a real improvement in performance.

This meant studies using a control group for comparison. Productivity can increase in an organization due to outside factors, such as technological improvements or changes in the general economic climate. To identify the effects of leadership practices on a work group, a study must include a control group — a part of the organization that is not exposed to the new leadership practice being studied or piloted. If the improved-leadership work group experiences a rise in productivity while the control group does not, it can be concluded that the new leadership skill or practice made a difference. This is a valuable finding; it means that you can use the proven technique and be confident that you will achieve a similar improvement in a new situation.

As I identified, compiled, and summarized these "hard data" studies, I discovered a whole new way of looking at leadership. Read the studies below and see if your conclusions match mine.

Two-Way Listening

One of the most intensively studied leadership improvement techniques has been training in the skill of listening. Ten hard-data studies produced startlingly similar conclusions: when team leaders, supervisors, and managers were trained to listen effectively, their subordinates became more productive, produced higher-quality work, and reduced waste and costs.[1] The overall performance improvement was measured at 10 percent. Among employees and work groups whose managers and supervisors did not receive listening skills training, there was no improvement.

Most of these managers were accustomed to supervising in a top-down manner, telling their subordinates what to do and not inviting questions or comments. Their subordinates were passive followers who contributed little or nothing; they were expected simply to obey orders and follow instructions — to maintain the status quo.

After these managers were trained to ask for and listen to their subordinates' ideas, leadership interactions became more collegial. Subordinates became active contributors. They brought their personal experience, insights, and strengths to bear on improving their work and the results. The investment in effort was not large; when leaders received only eight hours or so of training in interpersonal listening skills, their team members' productivity gradually increased by 10 percent or more over the next two to three months.

When I read this interpersonal listening training research, I recognized many of the ideas and practices. Early in my career, one cold November in Northfield, Massachusetts, I had participated in a similar program led by psychologist Robert R. Carkhuff. We had paired off in practice

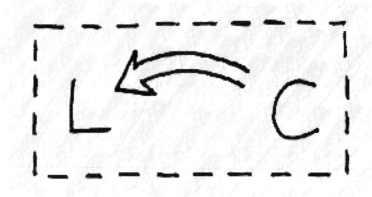

sessions to improve our communication skills. Our assignment was to listen to our counterpart and then summarize accurately what we were told.

I had great difficulty doing this. Rather than simply listening and then repeating and summarizing what my partner had said, I usually tried to find hidden meanings. I also felt compelled to offer advice, which, while well intentioned, was usually not helpful, because I had not listened carefully enough to what my partner was saying to me.

In short, when people in positions of authority listen to the ideas of subordinates, performance improves significantly. But this conclusion, as you are probably aware, goes against the cultural grain. When you see leaders portrayed in our media — novels, motion pictures, television shows — you see top-down leadership, with bold, decisive leaders holding the floor and starry-eyed, empty-headed followers listening. With such role models reinforcing traditional notions of authority, it's no wonder that leaders often talk when they should be listening.

Two-Way Performance Coaching

Like most leaders and managers, you probably conduct performance reviews with the individuals on your team. But do you know how to use these sessions to improve performance?

In one important study, supervisors were trained to facilitate structured, thirty-minute, one-on-one meetings with their contributors as discussions between equals on how they could improve performance. Control group leaders tried to improve working conditions on their own, rather than working with their contributors. The trained supervisors followed a five-step procedure that called for Side by Side involvement of contributors. Here's what happened during a typical session, with "Karen" as the leader and "Douglas" as the contributor:

1. Karen asked Douglas to state any concerns, dislikes, or expectations about his job, her job, and their current working relationship.

2. Karen suspended her own viewpoint and position of authority, and simply listened.

3. Karen checked her understanding of what Douglas said by summarizing his key points back to him.

4. Karen presented her expectations and concerns about her own performance, Douglas's performance, and their current working relationship.

5. Karen and Douglas together identified and concurred on actions to improve performance.

The key point in the structured discussion was the second item. Supervisors were taught to step outside their position of authority for the session and conduct the discussion as equals. The result was a 15 percent improvement in productivity, compared with control groups in which performance reviews were conducted traditionally, with supervisors rating subordinates from a position of authority.[2]

This study showed how average managers and supervisors could readily improve the productivity of their work teams. A follow-up study demonstrated that even greater improvements could be realized with supervisors who had poor relationships with their subordinates. Following the same training procedures as in the first study, these super-

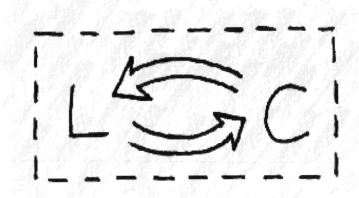

visors were taught to conduct mutual performance reviews with individuals with whom they were having the most problems. The result was an improvement in productivity that was greater than 15 percent — in fact, an increase in profits of $5 million for the company.[3]

How can changing the way a thirty-minute meeting is run improve the performance of a company by 15 percent or more? There are four key principles:

1. The interaction is two-way and mutual.

2. The conversation is structured.

3. The leader is trained and required to practice excellent interpersonal listening.

4. The leader's point of view, although presented after the contributor's, is equally important.

The research that holds up scientifically shows that the best, most effective relationship between the two participants is neither top-down nor bottom-up. Instead, it is a third way: a two-way, shared leadership. The leader asks for and listens to the ideas of the contributor. The leader does not, however, cede authority, but participates equally. Leader and contributor listen to each other; they share ideas on how to improve performance.

Side by Side Decision Making

If two-way, mutual interaction in one-on-one relationships has been shown to increase productivity, how about teams and work groups? The 1,200 studies I reviewed for an earlier book, *Breakthrough Teamwork,* as well as more recent work, have demonstrated the value of two-way, mutual interactions. Leaders and work teams that were trained to use improved listening techniques, two-way communication, and participative problem solving and decision making saw productivity increase 20 percent or more.[4]

Specifically, here's what happened when team leaders and supervisors asked for team members' ideas, rather than solving problems and making decisions on their own and then imposing them from above:

1. Team members showed greater commitment to team goals.

2. There was less conflict within teams.

3. Decisions were more creative and effective.

4. Problems were solved more creatively.

5. Planning improved.

6. Team members accepted and implemented changes more readily.

7. Work performance improved measurably.

In one study, work group productivity rose 20 percent when forty-minute group meetings were held every two weeks to discuss ways to improve performance. At first, the supervisor began the meetings by asking for team members' ideas and writing them down. After a while, team members began to take the initiative, with the supervisor participating as an equal. The result? The productivity of these teams increased by 20 percent at the same time that of two control groups declined. In addition, employee absentee rates in these teams fell below that of the organization as a whole.[5]

To see if shared group facilitation would continue to increase productivity after the first six months, the study was extended by a year. The work group's productivity did indeed continue to increase; after eighteen months, it was 50 percent higher than before the study began. Productivity continued to decline in the two control groups.

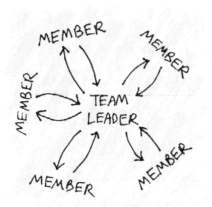

In a modern organization, work teams are the preferred way to coordinate all the interconnected work processes that are required to satisfy today's customers. The hard-data studies show that teams perform best when team members share the leadership and participate in making decisions. Mutual leadership encourages team members to think and to contribute ideas for solving problems and achieving goals. Tapping the knowledge and experience of everyone leads to improved performance, higher productivity, and increased profits.

Managers are less successful when they try to "sell and tell" the team members what to do. Selling and telling is a loser; two-way mutual sharing is a winner, every time.

The Pioneers

Many other authors have contributed ideas that could lead to leadership models other than top-down and bottom-up. The following tables summarize the contributions of the early thinkers and more recent ones.

Early Leadership Thinkers

Leadership Thinkers and Their Major Discoveries[6]

Significance of the Discoveries to Increased Productivity

G. Elton Mayo: Giving workers attention and a sense of belonging to a group increased productivity.

Creating a positive group dynamic in a work group requires planning and structure.

Peter Drucker. Considered the father of the field of management after publishing research on the effectiveness of General Motors.

Identified the importance of organizational leadership practices such as mission and strategy development.

Kurt Lewin. First to call leadership a two-way process; held that individual personality must be examined in the context of one's social group.

With Ronald Lippitt, did first research showing how authoritarian leadership could impair performance.

Douglas McGregor: Theory X, Theory Y. Theory X said that workers were motivated only by money and the threat of job loss. Theory Y was the discovery that most workers were also motivated by a supportive work climate, job challenge, recognition, and sense of accomplishment.

If workers were motivated by the work itself and other factors, then top-down treatment of the workers by bosses was not warranted. This research opened the door to motivating workers by considering the quality of their work environment, including how they were treated by their bosses and co-workers.

Robert Blake and Jane Mouton: *The Managerial Grid.* The management grid had two dimensions of leadership, managing the tasks or the work itself and managing the people who did the work.

The management grid elevated the importance of how supervisors and managers should treat the people they are supposed to lead.

Eric Trist: The Socio-Technical Method of Work Design. Workers have social needs at work. They want the ability to plan their workday with their co-workers and to communicate briefly throughout the day about progress and problems.

Trist and his fellow researchers discovered that there was greater productivity if the workers were placed in shared management teams in which they could plan and set their own daily production goals.

Both early and recent thinkers provide clues about new kinds of leadership that can enhance the performance of an organization. The systems models of Peter Senge, Margaret

Modern Leadership Thinkers

Leadership Thinkers and Their Major Discoveries[7]	Significance of the Discoveries to Increased Productivity
Tom Peters, Bob Waterman: *In Search of Excellence.* Eight characteristics of excellent companies include bias for action; close to the customer; autonomy & entrepreneurship; productivity through people; hands-on values; simple form & lean staff.	Leadership is more important than management in the excellent companies. Workers want leaders who provide a focused vision, recognize success, & promote innovation & creativity.
Bernard Bass: *Transformational Leadership.* Good leadership links with people's highest values & goals. Leaders provide goals that inspire people & provide them with new knowledge to achieve the goals & more.	Leadership can be more than a business transaction between leader & follower. Both can do & become more. The importance of goals & knowledge sharing are emphasized.
Stephen Covey: *The Seven Habits of Highly Effective People.* Described how people with strong personal & interpersonal leadership habits & skills are successful.	Importance of leaders having clear goals & desired outcomes, of interpersonal listening, & of win-win negotiation for personal & organizational productivity.
Peter Senge: *The Fifth Discipline.* Importance of systems thinking in preventing & solving organizational problems, empowered teams, & the creation of a learning organization inside every company.	Shared management teams can devise practices to increase productivity. Systems thinking is a tool leaders & teams could use to think about what is happening outside their immediate line of sight.
Margaret Wheatley: *Leadership and the New Science.* Understanding complex systems & chaos theory will help leaders understand how to intervene in their own organization.	Leaders succeed or fail within organizations composed of many elements, people, & interactions inside & outside. Lead by applying principles from natural complex systems.
Murray Bowen, Michael Kerr, Dan Papero: *Family and Natural Systems Theory.* Close human relationships can be understood as patterns of emotions & interactions. Psychology & management will become true sciences only when integrated with the discoveries of natural sciences such as biology & neurophysiology.	Leaders have reciprocal relationships with the people they work closest with. Leaders can create underfunctioning workers by doing the thinking & even some of the tasks of the workers. Leaders' emotional maturity & personal sense of direction influences the ability of work groups & organizations to handle crises.

Wheatley, and the Murray Bowen Natural Systems thinkers (Michael Kerr and Daniel Papero) are consistent with the hard-data research I have uncovered.

Leadership involves many components: leader, contributors, their interactions, and their relationships to team, department, organizational, and outside influences. What is needed is a systems model that describes how all these parts are intimately related. The chapters that follow will show you how to apply the Side by Side systems model to achieve higher performance — for yourself as a leader, for your contributors, and for your organization.

Side by Side Tips

Here, then, is what our research and experience tell us about the principles of Side by Side Leadership:

- By using good listening skills, you can increase the other person's performance by 10 percent.

- Using structured, two-way performance reviews, in which you and your contributor listen to each other, you can improve performance by 15 percent.

- By inviting contributors to present their ideas first, you can increase involvement and mutual respect.

- Telling followers what to do invites failure; encouraging contributors to share their ideas and knowledge brings success.

- Effective organization leaders are open to ideas from everyone — peers, subordinates, bosses, and outsiders.

- When leaders and work teams use two-way communication and participative problem solving and decision making, productivity increases 20 percent or more.

Chapter 3

The Name of the Third Way

Defining a New Model of Leadership That Increases Performance, Productivity, and Profit

Having plowed through thousands of research write-ups and absorbed the significance of the relatively few that had a scientific basis, I felt I had gathered enough information to answer my original question: "What leadership practices and skills could be taught to people that would make a positive difference?" In fact, I could even identify the simple, unifying idea that underlay the most successful of the leadership practices. The problem was, I didn't know what to call my discovery. "Mutual" leadership? That was close, but it didn't have the right ring to it.

Around this time, I attended a training session at the Bowen Center for the Study of the Family in Washington, D.C., to learn more about natural systems theory. One evening I went to dinner with a friend and colleague, Dr. Paul Radde. As friends will do, we took turns telling each other our problems and ideas.

In the good spirit of the evening, I threw my terminology problem out to Paul. What would be a good name for mutual leadership that wouldn't sound like behavioral science jargon? Paul listened politely. He agreed with me that I needed to draw a distinction from "top-down" and "bottom-up" leadership.

"How about Side by Side Leadership?" he offered. Immediately my mind filled with images of great leaders in world history who had led "side by side."

I thought of Martin Luther King Jr. leading his famous march for desegregation in Birmingham, Alabama, walking alongside women and men from all races and all walks of life. King's Side by Side Leadership conformed to the vision to which he gave his life, a future America in which all races could live and work together in peace and equality.

I remembered reading that George Washington, the first president of the United States, visited with each of his cabinet members to ask their advice before he made any important decision; that Mohandas Gandhi, the revered liberator of India, walked side by side with the other leaders of the independence movement to the Indian Ocean to protest the British monopoly on the sale of table salt. I also recalled the little-known fact that Albert Einstein, the twentieth century's most famous physicist, developed his theories of relativity working with two close colleagues around dining room tables and on walks.

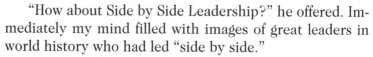

I thought of Martin Luther King Jr. walking alongside women and men from all races and all walks of life.

I was reminded of how Abraham Lincoln won the loyalty and love of the Union soldiers, who repaid him by keeping their nation undivided. In the early days of the Civil War, when even his own cabinet members dismissed him as incompetent, Lincoln was largely ignored by the troops when he went to visit General McClellan in the field. McClellan, an intelligent but fainthearted military leader, was well loved by his troops and the public — too popular for the president to fire despite numerous defeats.

Lincoln quietly made it known that soldiers were welcome to come visit him in the White House. When many took him up on this invitation, Lincoln would sit beside them on a velvet-padded wooden couch and talk over their fears and problems with them, or sometimes just listen.

Within a couple of years, thousands of soldiers had visited the president. Then, when he went to the battlefield and the troops cheered louder for him than for General McClellan, Lincoln knew he had turned the corner. General McClellan needed firing more urgently than ever, and that's what Lincoln did. This action led to the victories of General Ulysses S. Grant and the eventual defeat of the Confederacy.

When people walk side by side, they are journeying in the same direction together. When people work and plan side by side, they also face the same direction — their shared vision of the future.

A New Definition

Side by Side Leadership: what comes to your mind when you read this term? When I mention it to organizational leaders, many of them grasp the main idea immediately. Almost spontaneously, they begin to work side by side with others to set goals, plan work, solve problems, evaluate performance, draw up budgets, and create new ventures. They get out from behind their desks and join others around conference tables. They go where the work is being done. They ask contributors for ideas, listen to workers, and sometimes roll up their sleeves and go to work alongside them.

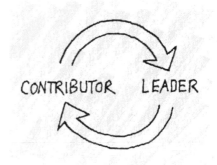

CONTRIBUTOR LEADER

If we are to begin the process of achieving a new model of leadership, we must get beyond thinking of leadership as a one-way process. One-way processes leave little room for actively involved contributors. I propose the following definition:

> Leadership is facilitating Side by Side relationships in pursuit of shared goals.

When I present this new definition to old-style, top-down bosses, their immediate reaction is often, "But my workers act like children! They have to be told what to do, and how to do it!"

"I agree with you," I respond. "That is exactly the problem we propose to solve with Side by Side Leadership."

The Bowen Center for the Study of the Family, in Washington, D.C., discovered that family and other close interpersonal relationships form natural systems. According to natural systems theory, as taught by Drs. Michael Kerr and Daniel Papero, current leaders of the interdisciplinary center, leader/follower or leader/contributor relationships are reciprocal. In the old, top-down model, the followers adapt to being told what to do at work and stop thinking for themselves. Often they resist; sometimes they rebel.

Natural systems theory predicts that if workers are treated as fully equal contributors in leadership processes, they will behave as such and work performance will improve. The hard-data research we have seen supports this prediction. Followers, when allowed or invited to participate in making decisions, invest themselves in the work and become contributors.

There are other conclusions we can draw from natural systems theory:

1. Leadership is an interactive process.

2. The kind of leadership that achieves dramatically improved performance is a two-way street.

3. Often the most effective way for leaders to influence subordinates is to change their own behavior.

4. Contributors have a greater positive impact on results than followers.

Thus the leader's role must become one of facilitating and coordinating the two-way influence process. Effective leaders get others to work together to achieve extraordinary results. They listen and respond to their contributors, and they share leadership with them.

Natural systems theory also proposes that relationships inside the organization are influenced by what happens both outside and inside. The effective Side by Side leader is aware of all these influences on the team and organization and knows that front-line people — the employees who are in daily contact with customers and suppliers — are often the first to discover new opportunities and threats to the organization.

By maintaining a two-way dialogue, Side by Side leaders and their contributors can respond quickly to changes without losing sight of their goals.

Leadership vs. Management

We have traditionally expected people in management positions to be leaders as well. However, the statistics tell us that being a manager does not equate to being a leader. They also show that people who have no position in the organizational hierarchy *can* be leaders.

What is the difference between a manager and a leader?

- Managers influence results from their position at the top of the organizational hierarchy; leaders can affect results anywhere in the organization.

- Managers make their presence known by boxes on an organization chart; leaders, by their breakthrough results and their facilitating presence throughout the organization.

- Managers optimize existing resources; leaders create new resources.

- Managers improve efficiency; leaders improve effectiveness.

Managers influence results only through lines of authority. Leaders can affect results anywhere in the organization.

A fundamental difference in the new organizational structure is the dramatic loss of managerial authority and control. Today, when commerce and competition move fast, hierarchical management does not work. Top-down management is no longer the best way to influence an organizational outcome.

Many executives state that they want everyone in the organization to act as a leader — to use initiative, take responsibility, and be accountable. This means that everyone is expected to be on the alert for trends in new products and services, as well as for competitive risks. At Intel, for example, anyone could e-mail CEO Andy Grove with a problem, an insight, or a trend. Grove knew that people at

Major Successful Organizational Trends	
Changes in Business Environment	Changes Required in Organization Form
Global competition	Partnerships, alliances, virtual organizations
Global customers	Integrated supplier value chains
More accessible information & knowledge	Learning organizations, cross-functional knowledge worker teams
Rapidly improving & changing products & services	Customers on teams & involved in new product & service development
Business growing & contracting 20-40% per year	Rapid downsizing, outsourcing, leasing, & renting employees vs. employing
Knowledge economy as well as industrial & service economies	Access to new & best knowledge immediately & consistently
Decentralized empowerment	Smaller profit & loss centers, self-managed work teams, shared-management work teams

the edges of his organization would spot early trends before he or any other headquarters executive became aware of them. The spectacular success of his company speaks for Grove's leadership skills.

The Evolving Organization

Adapting to rapidly changing national and global business environments, organizations have changed both in form and in function. Global companies, not tied to any particular country or region, can form anywhere, gather the necessary resources, and coordinate production and marketing across oceans. Corporations lease or rent workers, rather than hiring them directly, and organize everyone into self-managed and shared-management teams. The stable, long-term, hierarchical corporate structure has been replaced by highly flexible organizations like Dell Computer, which reorganizes several times a year to meet changing needs.

The traditional pattern of horizontal or vertical integration, with subsidiaries owned or controlled by the core company, is being supplanted by the virtual corporation, consisting of joint ventures and partnerships. In this system, the partners in the extended enterprise are as important as the core in achieving the company's business goals. The business is only as successful as the weakest link in the chain that runs from its suppliers to its customers.

In this new business environment, the old vertical, hierarchical leadership models do not work. The organization of the future must be highly interactive; it must work horizontally with its customers, suppliers, research organizations, and alliance partners.

Of all the organizational innovations of the past ten years, shared-management teams are the most likely to endure. In terms of their effectiveness at improving performance, they have been compared to the invention of the assembly line. Some groups of employees, it has been shown, can manage themselves better than the managers who used to direct them.

Side by Side Leadership is the key to maximizing the effectiveness of empowered workers and shared-management teams. With the rise of knowledge workers and increased availability of knowledge, more and more organizations are finding that top-down leadership simply no longer works. How can a manager order her subordinates to do a job in a particular way when they know how to do the work better than she does? Leaders must learn and practice Side by Side behaviors that promote productivity in themselves and their workers.

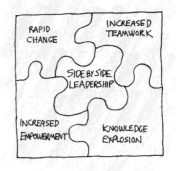

In the jigsaw puzzle formed by rapid changes in the business environment, more teamwork, greater worker empowerment, and increased worker knowledge, Side by Side Leadership fits with all the other pieces to promote outstanding performance by all.

Many managers I trained in high-tech companies (Dell, Motorola, and Texas Instruments) began as top-down bosses. One manager in particular, whose department had achieved 5 to 7 percent improvements year after year, was a hard worker himself, typically coming to work before 7:00 AM and staying on the job past 7:00 PM. Like many high-tech managers, he was tough and smart. He challenged me: Why should he change the very leadership behaviors that had gotten him promoted?

I told the manager I was not trying to take away his fact-based approach to decisions or his desire for people to be accountable. I simply wanted him to try some new ways of working with his people, of making his interactions more horizontal and two-way. The fact that the skills I recommended were based on hard-data research persuaded him to give the Side by Side Leadership approach a try.

I worked hard in the training and coaching sessions with him and his supervisors. We had many discussions, some of them heated, about whether or not workers were intrinsically lazy. After only a few months of using Side by Side Leadership, the productivity of his department soared 30 percent. This manager became a believer, and his team's performance continued to grow. He received promotion after promotion and became an industry leader.

The table on page 49 compares top-down and Side by Side interactions in each of eight typical leadership situations and summarizes the benefits of Side by Side Leadership. The improvement percentages reflect increases in productivity or profits according to hard-data research studies.

Before and After

This book is based on not only the hard-data research summarized above, but also my own first-hand observations — the success stories of several thousand leaders trained in Side by Side Leadership principles and skills. I documented the performance of leaders, teams, and organizations before and after leadership training.

Top-Down vs. Side by Side Leadership

Leadership Interaction	Top-Down Leadership	Side by Side Leadership	Benefits of Side by Side Leadership
Any interaction	Boss does most of the talking.	Leader listens & checks understanding to find out what contributor is saying.	Leader understands contributor better. Contributor feels respected. Performance improves 10%.
One-on-one meeting to clarify job roles & expectations	Boss tells subordinate his job tasks.	Leader asks contributor for her expectations, listens, checks understanding, then presents own expectations.	Leader can acknowledge areas of agreement & focus on differences. Contributor shares how leader can be more helpful. Performance improves 15–20%.
Solving a problem	Boss tells subordinates his solution.	Leader first asks contributors for their solutions.	More & better solutions; greater support for implementation.
Making a decision	Boss tells subordinates her decision.	Leader asks for options, discusses pros & cons with contributors; together they select the best course.	More creative & effective decisions; better team member acceptance & implementation; improved work performance.
Developing & implementing project plan	Boss develops, distributes plan; assigns responsibilities.	Leader asks all to list potential action steps; seeks consensus on major tasks; asks for volunteers to track tasks & ensure completion.	Superior planning; team member acceptance & implementation; improved work performance.
Enhancing work performance, reengineering work process	Boss tells employees how to improve their work.	Leader solicits and listens to employees' suggestions for improving performance; helps move ideas to action.	Work group productivity improves 20–50%.
Developing organizational values & vision	Manager or management group sets values & vision alone.	Leader discovers values of employees, customers, shareholders; develops overlapping values, which influence direction.	Profitability increases 750% over 11 years.
Setting goals	Supervisor gives each person written goals.	Leader & contributors set goals together; discuss importance of goals to organization.	Goal achievement improves 20–70% annually; improved performance in other areas.

The "before" picture was a chaotic scene of crisis management. It featured stressed-out managers and supervisors rushing around like firefighters in a disaster zone, putting out one blaze after another. They worked long days, carrying on their shoulders the full weight of responsibility for success, while their employees trampled them in their haste to leave work on time. In both group meetings and one on one, managers did most of the talking, sometimes yelling at subordinates; workers walked away grumbling. Workers hid problems from their superiors, sometimes serious problems of the kind that ultimately cost one organization $1 million.

With Side by Side Leadership in practice, the picture changed dramatically. Instead of rushing around in a panic, leaders walked around calmly, greeting contributors cordially, listening to workers' concerns, discussing new ideas with people who were no longer afraid to offer them — ideas worth millions of dollars to the company.

Meetings became lively, creative forums. Everybody participated in solving problems and improving critical work processes. All shared the responsibility for achieving work group goals because all had been involved in developing them. Workers shared day-to-day management responsibilities, allowing leaders to concentrate on more strategic opportunities. Mediocre leaders became good leaders; good leaders became world-class leaders and even taught my colleagues and me new ideas about leadership. Individual teams performed 20 to 30 percent better. Over two or three years, the confluence of these productivity streams produced a 100 to 300 percent rise in organizational profits.

In her September 2000 address in Boston to her fellow CEOs, Hewlett-Packard's Carly Fiorina called for a new type of leadership: "Finally, leadership in the Digital Renaissance will be about the realization that everyone on this earth is born with the potential to lead. This will be a deep and fundamental shift — a shift worth celebrating."[1]

Chapter 4

Spheres of Influence

How the Five Spheres of Leadership Define the Individual Leader and Work Together to Improve the Organization

Leaders are different. Even the greatest leaders in history differed from each other in significant ways. Some, like Gandhi, inspired others through their personal integrity and passion; others, like Einstein, were influential by virtue of their intellect and knowledge. All leaders possess the same qualities in different measures, different combinations. It would be unrealistic to expect any leader, even the greatest, to be strong in all ways of influencing others.

The Five Spheres

Side by Side Leadership recognizes five distinct aspects of leadership that work in combination to define an individual leadership style. We call these the "five spheres of influence." Understanding these spheres, recognizing how each contributes to the overall strength of individual and organizational leadership, makes it possible to optimize one's own leadership style. Anyone who is motivated can analyze her own leadership capabilities and use them side by side with others to create outstanding performance.

These are the five spheres of influence of Side by Side Leadership:[1]

Personal leadership. This is the one element that all leaders must have in order for Side by Side Leadership to work. If a leader does not have strong values and direction, followers will not become Side by Side contributors. Conversely, a high-profile leader with integrity, passion, and commitment can influence others simply by living and working in harmony with his values and goals. Contributors learn to trust a personal leader who shows integrity and ethics; they walk alongside the leader even when the road is rocky and the direction uncertain.

Knowledge leadership. Most people are easily influenced by the emotions of others. In Side by Side Leadership, knowledge leadership is a force that tempers and guides these emotional influences. Knowledge leaders take into account the best and most recent information, which enables other leaders and contributors to make the correct decision regarding any problem or opportunity.

In the 1990s, it was faddish to be a "knowledge worker" — an engineer, chemist, lawyer, accountant, or other user of specialized information. But this term is misleading; the simple truth is that all workers, including those in service industries and manufacturing, use specialized knowledge to do their jobs. Knowledge workers are needed in every corner of the organization. The factory worker who reduces costs by applying knowledge and experience to just-in-time inventory methods is as much a knowledge worker as is a computer programmer.

Interpersonal leadership. This is the influence a leader exerts person to person. It is the most intimate and direct of the five spheres of leadership influence, operating in both one-on-one and group interactions. Performance research has shown that a Side by Side interpersonal leadership approach can increase contributors' work performance 10 to 20 percent. Side by Side interpersonal leadership training teaches effective ways of listening, speaking, and coaching individuals and groups.

Team leadership. Along with the growth of jobs requiring specialized knowledge there has been a corresponding rise in work that is highly interdependent. Most tasks in organizations must be coordinated with other work done either inside or outside the organization. Team leaders are key coordinators, linking individual and team performance and goals to the organization's goals, mission, vision, and values. Side by Side team leadership transforms work groups, which are often teams in name only, into consistently high-performing teams.

Individuals on a team form a team interaction field, one of the many interaction fields that make up an organization. Skilled team leaders lead side by side with their team members, the team sponsor, and the managers and supervisors from other interaction fields. The research shows that when leaders train and require the whole team to share in leading the team (including its meetings), the result is a 25 to 70 percent improvement in performance.

Organizational leadership. Leading an organization or part of an organization requires a different set of skills than team, knowledge, or interpersonal leadership. It involves understanding organizations as systems that interact in specific ways within themselves and with other organizations. Organizational leadership can either enhance or hinder the performance of everyone. Side by Side organizational leaders influence all internal leaders and contributors to uphold values and achieve visionary goals. They also work side by side with leaders of other organizations to achieve mutual goals.

Working Together

To understand how the five spheres of influence interact, take a moment to study the "five spheres" figure. The personal leadership element is at the center of the figure; this symbolizes the central importance of personal influence in Side by Side Leadership. It means that your leadership, to be effective, must be in harmony with your own values, personal purpose, and goals. All the other spheres of influence, all other leadership skills, emanate from and interact through this personal core.

Each of the five spheres of influence complements and supports the others. For example, to be a knowledge leader one must acquire knowledge. Acquiring knowledge often necessitates using interpersonal skills to gain access to other leaders' knowledge — that is, to learn from others. Later, applying this knowledge to improve a work group's performance requires team leadership.

Most people have one or two leadership skills that are better developed than the others. The following examples will help you recognize leaders who excel in certain spheres of influence. Notice how each leader uses his or her skills and interests to facilitate Side by Side Leadership. (These leaders are actual people; names have been changed to protect their privacy.)

Personal Leadership

Jay's forte is in the personal leadership sphere of influence. He has four life goals:

1. To stay in good physical shape by making a three-mile run four to five times a week.

2. To spend time and share interests with each member of his family.

3. To support his own growth and learning, as well as those of all the people he interacts with.

4. To lead his organization in achieving its goals.

Jay is totally focused on those goals. He does not waste time watching television or in other nonproductive activities. Each day, including weekends, he spends at least 90 percent of his time in pursuit of one or another of his four goals.

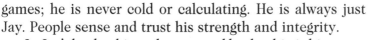

Jay brings this rock-steady strength to bear in interactions with the hundred or so people he leads at work. If he hears or sees something that does not fit his organization's goals or values, Jay addresses the issue immediately, but calmly and with respect for the other person. Though he interacts every week with more politicians than most of us see in our lifetime, he does not play political games; he is never cold or calculating. He is always just Jay. People sense and trust his strength and integrity.

In Jay's leadership style, personal leadership is his strongest competency. The Side by Side Leadership diagram indicates this with a large personal leadership sphere.

Knowledge Leadership

Any organization that expects to compete successfully in today's rapidly changing global economy must have access to knowledge leadership.[2] Without knowledge leadership, leaders and contributors would have to make important technical decisions based entirely on personal relationships and feelings. This is not a good way to run a business if your business is building spacecraft, bridges, computer chips, or even a good-tasting, crispy taco. You need theoretical knowledge and empirical data.

Anthony's genius is in marketing information technology products and services such as computers and software. Among the high management positions he has held is that of a marketing coordinator reporting to vice presidents. Anthony has two major work goals:

1. To fulfill what is asked of him.
2. To build his store of knowledge.

Anthony sees power in every scrap of information that comes his way. For example, he learns that one overnight express-mail service has just announced that it can guarantee two-day service anywhere in the United States, a capability that gives it a competitive advantage over other services. What is the key to this breakthrough? Anthony, whose store of knowledge includes logistics technology, surmises that the overnight service company has upgraded its computer-based package-tracking system to allow destina-

tion codes to be entered at the point of pickup. Other airmail cargo companies are now vulnerable — until they can acquire a comparably effective system. This is a goal that Anthony's company can help them attain. Anthony makes his first phone contact with one of those companies that same day.

Knowledge leaders have a passion for learning and putting their knowledge to use. They study voraciously in their area of expertise, even using their downtime to acquire more information. Perhaps not so obviously, they organize the information. Some keep paper or electronic files of key information; others set up a system to cross-index it. Anthony does both, and he also diagrams predictive models of what is happening in key information technology businesses. When a company announces a major innovation, Anthony can immediately draw up a table of winners and losers.

Anthony's influence pattern reflects his competency in knowledge leadership. He has a secondary strength in organizational leadership, which makes him a key person in analyzing and managing business threats and opportunities for his company.

Interpersonal Leadership

Leaders who are strong in the interpersonal leadership sphere have excellent listening skills that they use to help others. This is an important leadership skill because, as our research has shown, effective listening is fundamental to raising productivity.

In his first job, Daniel taught at a high school where all the other teachers had at least twenty years' experience. In his first weeks, Daniel's listening skills helped him learn and remember his colleagues' names, interests, and concerns. They, in turn, liked talking to Daniel because he actually heard, thought about, and responded to what they told him.

The secretaries and janitors liked Daniel, too. He paid attention to them, showed interest in their work and concerns, and was able to learn from them. They told him, among other things, that although the school had an excellent library of films, none of the teachers used them because no one knew how to run a projector. Sensing an opportunity to help, Daniel volunteered to come to other teachers' classrooms between classes and load the films for them.

Daniel made friends with a special-projects coordinator at the local university who had government grant money to fund on-site teaching improvement seminars. Daniel's school qualified, and Daniel was offered a $1,000 fee to coordinate the program at his school. At the next faculty meeting, Daniel recommended the program but offered to split the coordination duties — and the fee — with the other teachers. They enthusiastically agreed. The seminar was a success, and Daniel gained new respect and influence.

At the beginning of Daniel's second year of teaching, the administration selected Daniel to develop and manage a new program for problem students, a position that brought him more money and prestige. Rather than being jealous of Daniel, as you might expect, the other teachers were supportive. He enjoyed continued success in that job, as well as in subsequent positions. Wherever he worked, Daniel developed many mutually supportive relationships — both professional and personal.

In Daniel's leadership pattern, his primary competencies lie in the area of interpersonal leadership. Daniel's personal leadership influence is also large, because it is part of his personal philosophy to help others. Both in being a teacher and in helping other teachers, Daniel has always acted in accordance with his personal values and goals in life.

Team Leadership

Essential in any large endeavor is the ability to coordinate and support the efforts of groups of people. As work becomes more complex and interconnected, every successful worker needs to gain competence in team leadership.

Linda was a key contributor on a team of engineers engaged in product development. She always finished her work on time and eagerly helped other team members with theirs. But she knew something was wrong. Over time, the team's morale plummeted and turnover became a problem. Even the team leader's work began to deteriorate.

The team leader, a nationally recognized scientist, often confided in Linda his disappointment in other team members. Linda would defend the team, mentioning its positive achievements, and would urge the leader to take a more positive attitude toward them. But it became obvious that the team leader was more interested in making new discoveries on his own than in helping other team members, to whom he paid little attention. His "weekly" team meetings were hit or miss, more on the order of one every month or so. He didn't seem to realize that his lack

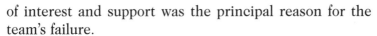

of interest and support was the principal reason for the team's failure.

Finally, in an especially open and candid discussion with the team leader, Linda said, "Would you like for me to give it a try? Let me take over facilitating the team." The scientist agreed.

Linda began holding weekly team meetings on schedule. She arranged structured team-skills training. Soon the team began setting goals, developing creative work plans, and leading their own meetings, rotating leadership to give each person a share in the responsibility and outcome. They learned team decision-making skills; they began to collaborate on important decisions.

The emotional turmoil gradually subsided. Team members went on to form sub-teams; they proposed and successfully implemented many new projects that benefited the organization. Annual turnover dropped from 30 to 5 percent.

Although she was not the designated team leader, Linda used a variety of team leadership skills to solve the team's problems. She communicated high performance expectations to everyone, but she gave team members encouragement and support, providing them with technical training and other resources to promote excellent performance. Poor performance was addressed promptly but constructively, without rancor. Most significant was her success in improving the lead scientist's productivity and his teamwork skills. Linda's success caught the attention of other leaders. She began to receive recognition and regular promotions.

Linda's leadership pattern emphasizes her strength in the team leadership sphere. It also shows a secondary emphasis in personal leadership because of her adherence to one of her personal goals: to help other people.

Organizational Leadership

Many leaders excel in one of the above four leadership spheres of influence, get promoted to the organizational leadership sphere, and immediately find themselves in unfamiliar territory. They may not have organizational leadership skills or know how to use them.

Gene was different, even in his first job as an engineer for an electric utility company. He did his work well, but he was also a sponge for information about the organization. He was curious about his boss's goals, his boss's boss's goals, and the company's overall goals and vision for the future. As he did his work, he took care to ensure that it helped his boss's priorities.

With his carefully cultivated sense of the organization's direction, he knew which special projects were critical and which projects and meetings were a waste of time. Working on projects that implemented large-scale organizational changes, he took the time to ask people what they liked and did not like about the changes; he knew the importance of forming a consensus.

Company executives took notice of Gene's service as a team member and presenter. They also noticed when he scheduled short but well-organized meetings with them to present preliminary project results or recommendations. This gave Gene special access to the executives, who felt comfortable sharing with him their dreams and concerns for the organization. Gene began to form a mental map of the key forces and personalities in the organization, and to foresee how they might work together in achieving the organization's goals.

Gene was promoted twice as frequently as others in his peer group. He liked the extra money, but what really got him excited was the chance to help the organization reach its goals. This compelling desire led him to study everything that had a bearing on the company's overall success. Gene developed relationships with associates in other companies. He read industry reports and trends. He began to understand how changes in customers' needs, vendors' capabilities, competitors' intentions, and government regulations affected his company's future. His thirst for knowledge and his comprehensive understanding of his organization and his industry helped him anticipate and prepare for major changes in the electric utility business.

Whatever new responsibilities Gene was given, he achieved success beyond anyone's expectations. Gene was ultimately appointed CEO of his company, capping a successful and distinguished career.

Gene was one of those exceptional leaders with a set of abilities and interests in organizational leadership. His leadership pattern shows a large knowledge element as well, because he constantly sought and acquired knowledge that was useful to his company's success.

Why "One Size Fits All" Doesn't

In the Side by Side Leadership model, each of the five individuals described above is considered a successful leader. Each was successful, however, in a different way, with a unique set of abilities and interests, a unique pattern of leadership spheres of influence. There is no single combination of attributes that makes a good leader; it depends on the time, the place, the organization, and the individual.

This is good news for you and for me. It means we can become successful leaders in our own way without necessarily having to be like our boss or any other leader in the organization. We can assemble our own set of leadership skills and tools and be our own kind of leader.

I wish I had known this a long time ago. I was once a manager for an executive who was totally different from me. I had the mistaken notion that if I wanted to move higher in the organization, I would have to be like him. And I didn't like the way he led. I have since learned. And you can learn — to be the leader you want to be.

Why do most current leadership programs fail? Why do they not create leaders who can regularly and repeatedly produce great results in their organizations? Most fail for two reasons. First, they are based on the old definition of leadership: influencing others through top-down behaviors. Second, the programs are designed to turn each individual into an exemplar created from a single list of leadership qualities.

Many managers on the brink of being fired are sent for a week to a leadership development program. They return talking a good story, but their behavior is not consistent with their talk. Inevitably, the old problems return. The organization is worse off than before, because the program has created the superficial appearance that the leader has improved. Even though no real improvement occurs and the organization continues to deteriorate, higher management still defers taking action; they believe that, sooner or later, the benefits of the leadership development program are bound to kick in.

> We can become successful leaders in our own way without necessarily having to be like our boss or any other leader.

A homogenous model of leadership, one that requires all individuals to subscribe to a single formula regardless of where they are in their careers, is a model that is bound to fail. It is more effective to develop leaders' skills in the spheres of influence that are most critical in their current position. The company doesn't need Superman; it just needs knowledge leadership here, organizational leadership there, and so forth. Think of it as "just-in-time" training in Side by Side Leadership.

Side by Side Leadership allows for an almost infinite variety of leadership patterns and styles. However, as symbolized by the leadership pattern diagram, personal leadership is always at the center. All spheres of influence are tied to the leader's personal values and goals. Many leaders fail because their leadership responsibilities or practices do not fit with their personal values or goals. They feel frustrated, anxious, and irritable at work. This book will show you how to avoid this kind of misalignment; it will help you keep all components of your leadership working together for maximum effect.

Informal Leaders and Contributors

The Side by Side Leadership model recognizes that some of the most important leaders in an organization can be contributors who do not hold management titles. For instance,

Daniel, the teacher discussed earlier, was strong in interpersonal and personal leadership, even as an individual contributor without a formal title. The same is true of Linda, whose team leadership skills saved her team despite the failure of its nominal leader.

A study of one very accomplished work team, conducted at the National Aeronautics and Space Administration during the Apollo space missions to the moon, found that the most important leaders were not the 20 supervisors but the most technically competent of the 117 contributors.[3] What was true for the Apollo program has become even more relevant for today's organizations. Individual contributors can, and should, be leaders, too.[4] This diagram, for example, describes an individual contributor who holds no management position, but whose principal leadership influence comes through his knowledge. In many high-tech enterprises, contributors often become de facto leaders, and later titled executives, because of their demonstrated knowledge or technical expertise.

In this example, the next most important influence shown is in team leadership, because this knowledge leader is playing a positive role in a team. Many engineers and technicians are not recruited into either organizational or informal leadership roles because they do not function well on teams. Training and coaching to make them more effective as team leaders can increase the effectiveness of their knowledge and produce better team and organizational performance. It can also pave the way for promotions.

A Coherent Model of Leadership

The Side by Side Leadership model is a useful, innovative way of thinking about the elements of effective leadership. The diagrams should be thought of as a convenient way of categorizing the values, skills, and practices of effective

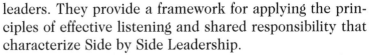

leaders. They provide a framework for applying the principles of effective listening and shared responsibility that characterize Side by Side Leadership.

Although individual patterns vary widely, each of the five spheres of influence is important to leadership success. The interactions between them are key factors in their effectiveness. For example, when knowledge leaders improve in the interpersonal leadership sphere, they can communicate better and derive greater benefit from their knowledge. Similarly, effective team leaders can help connect the visionary goals of organizational leaders to the grass-roots teams.

Side by Side Tips

Keep in mind these three basic facts about the leadership patterns used in the Side by Side Leadership model:

- Leaders can succeed with different patterns of abilities and interests.

- Each leader requires different sets of abilities and skills in the different spheres of influence and in different stages of his career. The necessary abilities should be mapped to the organization's position and needs.

- Individual contributors can and must be leaders!

Part

II

The Seven Principles of Side by Side Leadership

The next seven chapters present seven major principles to guide you as you transform your leadership interactions into outstanding results for your team and organization. Each principle alone will help you improve your overall leadership. But there's synergy here to be tapped; the seven principles will have a more dramatic impact if you use them all in every planning session, every team strategy meeting, every one-on-one interaction that you are involved in.

The Seven Principles

1. **Two-Way Street:** Two-Way Communication, Power Sharing, and Teamwork Feed High Performance

2. **Interaction Fields:** Bridging Resources across Internal and External Interaction Fields Grows New Assets

3. **Visionary Goals:** Shared Visionary Goals Magnetically Pull Innovative Thinking and Increased Productivity

4. **Focused Creativity:** Fostering Outside-the-Box Thinking Produces Breakthrough Ideas

5. **Structured Participation:** Facilitating Total Participation Arouses Extraordinary Commitment

6. **Proven Knowledge:** Filtering Creative Ideas through the Sieve of Knowledge and Experience Separates Out Workable Innovations

7. **Transferred Authority:** Transferring Decision-Making Power Jump-Starts Action on New Ideas

Chapter 5

Principle 1:

Two-Way Street

Two-Way Communication, Power Sharing, and Teamwork Feed High Performance

Side by Side Leadership is a two-way street in three important ways:

- Side by Side leaders are two-way in their communication. This results in more ideas and knowledge being used in every meeting and conversation. A key skill for leaders to learn is how to listen more effectively.

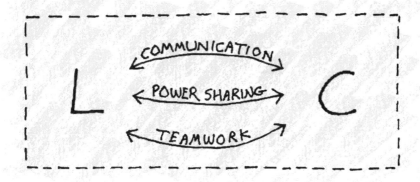

How Side By Side Leadership Is Two-Way		
Activity	Top-Down	Two-Way
Communication	DOMINATING: Only the boss talks; follower is supposed to listen & obey	INTERACTIVE: Leader & contributor both talk, share their thinking, listen, & use each other's ideas
Power Sharing	AUTHORITARIAN: Boss forces decisions on followers	PARTICIPATIVE: Leader shares decision-making power with contributor
Teamwork	COMPETITIVE: Boss competes with followers for personal gain; followers resist	COOPERATIVE: Contributor & leader help each other

- Side by Side leaders and contributors are two-way in sharing power and decision-making authority, and in asking for each other's input on key decisions.

- Side by Side Leadership is also two-way in cooperation. Leaders help contributors and contributors help leaders. Information, ideas, and teamwork must flow freely in both directions for effective leadership.

Two-Way Communication

A Side by Side leader asks for and listens to contributors' ideas, knowing that contributors have knowledge resources that may prove valuable to the company. This show of respect, in turn, makes the contributor receptive to the leader's ideas. Two-way communication promotes the creation of shared goals, along with new ideas on how to achieve them.

Side by Side leaders lead more by listening than by talking. It sometimes takes a lot of listening to draw out the thinking of contributors who are not accustomed to being heard. Top-down, authoritarian leaders listen to only a few — mostly those in authority above them. The best Side by Side leaders listen to diverse voices and benefit from their combined wisdom, knowledge, and experience.

Here's a quick rule of thumb to gauge whether you're in a top-down situation. The next interaction you observe, whether a group meeting or a face-to-face talk, notice how long the leader talks and how long other people talk. Does the boss do most of the talking? Top-down bosses talk 70 percent of the time or more, leaving followers little or no time to present their ideas.

It's interesting to observe how people behave when one person dominates a discussion. Steve, for example, is a pretty good Side by Side leader most of the time, but sometimes in a meeting he gets anxious and dominates the discussion. The more he talks, the more his listeners express their discomfort — through their body language. They cough nervously, cross their arms, squirm in their chairs. Steve unconsciously picks up on their nervousness; this increases his anxiety, and he talks even more. Steve can go on talking for thirty minutes or more, which may not seem like a long time unless you multiply thirty wasted minutes by fourteen people who are sitting, squirming, and "listening."

Fortunately there is a quick way to shift the one-way communication back to two-way. One person says, "Steve, let me see if I understand what you're saying," then goes on to summarize for everybody the main points that Steve is trying to make. This person talks concisely but slowly, not as though she is trying to wrest control of the meeting from Steve. Steve, however, stops talking and begins listening, which shifts him to a two-way mode. The whole group listens, too. After the other person finishes talking, Steve either concurs with the summary or goes on to clarify.

In the field of speech and communication, a one-way presentation of information with no interaction or follow-up is not considered true communication. Two-way communication gets contributors intellectually engaged in discussions. Contributors whose ideas and opinions are

Side by Side leaders listen to diverse voices and benefit from their combined wisdom, knowledge, and experience.

> **HOW TO LEAD BY LISTENING**
>
> 1. DURING A LEADER-CONTRIBUTOR INTERACTION, THE CONTRIBUTOR PRESENTS AN IDEA, A PROBLEM, OR A CRITICISM.
> 2. RATHER THAN ANALYZE THE STATEMENT OR INTERJECT HER OWN IDEA, THE LEADER LISTENS CAREFULLY AND THINKS ABOUT WHAT THE CONTRIBUTOR IS SAYING.
> 3. WHEN THE CONTRIBUTOR FINISHES SPEAKING, THE LEADER SUMMARIZES WHAT SHE HAS HEARD AND ASKS IF THIS IS WHAT THE CONTRIBUTOR MEANT.
> 4. THE CONTRIBUTOR REPLIES, "THAT'S RIGHT," OR GOES ON TO CLARIFY.

respected, and who know they are expected to express them, do not mentally "check out" of a meeting. And when communication is two-way, the listener can offer the leader feedback about what was heard. Feedback makes it more likely that the listener will take away from the interaction what the leader intended.

In research conducted on improving leadership, one of the most frequently studied techniques has been training to improve listening skills. The results of ten control-group studies (discussed in chapter 2), conducted in a variety of organizations and locations across the United States, led to a surprising conclusion: the one thing that consistently improved the performance of contributors was listening training — for the leader!

In these studies, leaders were instructed to listen and try to understand what was being said, then paraphrase what they heard to check their understanding. The result? Some managers had great difficulty, at first, accurately hearing and summarizing what was said. People with advanced degrees who could understand university professors had trouble accurately listening to subordinates and peers. Rather than simply listening, they kept interrupting, analyzing the speaker's statements or trying to give advice.

Over some eight hours of training and testing, supervisors gradually learned to listen more attentively and "play back" messages more accurately. Then they returned to their organizations. Follow-up studies were conducted — which revealed an almost magical transformation. The productivity of the contributors whose leaders received the training gradually increased over the next two to three months, while the performance of control groups in the same organizations remained unchanged or even declined.[1]

Why "magical"? Because the leaders did not influence contributors in any traditional way, such as directly telling them what to do. All the leaders did was listen better and demonstrate respect for contributors' ideas and opinions.

The leader who listens gains a better understanding of the contributor's thinking and attitudes. This, in turn, changes the contributor's attitude toward the leader. The contributor feels respected because the leader patiently listens to him. The leader, in turn, gains respect from the contributor. Mutual respect brings an improved flow of information and potential breakthrough ideas.

Two-Way Power Sharing

Side by Side Leadership is also a two-way street when it comes to sharing decision-making power. When a leader involves contributors in making an important decision, the contributors become better motivated, more cooperative, and more inclined to help implement the decision.

Sharing decision-making authority takes more time up front. For important decisions to be made in an hourlong meeting, leaders should spend another hour planning the session. The extra time will result in increased contributor commitment extending over many forty-hour weeks; research also shows that it will raise the organization's performance by 25 percent or more in terms of productivity, quality, and efficiency.[2]

The leader who shares power does not necessarily simply go along with whatever the contributors decide. Different leaders may share power in different measures,

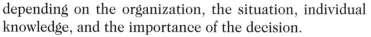

depending on the organization, the situation, individual knowledge, and the importance of the decision.

There are basically three levels of power sharing, each of which has the virtue of increasing mutual commitment for implementation:

Level 1: Contributors provide ideas to the leader. The leader asks contributors to share their ideas and discuss the pros and cons of the options. Contributors' ideas are written down, and the leader considers them when making the decision. Contributors' power is limited to having input and debating alternatives. The leader makes the decision alone.

Level 2: Contributors participate in the process. Leader and contributors collaborate by brainstorming and evaluating alternatives. If a consensus is not reached, the leader makes the final decision. Leaders share most of the power but retain the final say.

Level 3: Contributors and leaders share equally in the decision. Leader and contributors go through the decision-making process to arrive at a consensus, working together until everyone can support the decision. Leaders share all of their power with contributors; no decision is implemented until all can support it.

A leader may use different levels of power sharing for different kinds of decisions. For most decisions, one vice president of manufacturing used level 3 power sharing in team meetings or in one-on-one interactions with his managers and supervisors. However, he kept level 2 for two important decision categories in which he had a lot of expertise: organizational structure and communication with customers and other executives outside manufacturing. Some might say he was not leading side by side; but he did share power completely in all other decisions, and even in these two special areas he asked for and listened to the ideas of others. The vice president himself had led his organization into implementing shared-management teams, and he believed in practicing what he preached. In twelve months, the productivity of his manufacturing division increased 25 percent.

Two-Way Teamwork

Most people think of a team as many people working toward a common goal under an outside person — a leader. However, in Side by Side Leadership, a team can consist of merely a leader and a contributor, sharing work and decisions equally in pursuit of a common goal. In fact, I've experienced and observed great success in such teams.

Leaders demonstrate two-way teamwork, and Side by Side Leadership as well, when they roll up their sleeves and help their contributors do the work. They can help by providing tools, equipment, knowledge, and sometimes an extra pair of hands. In turn, contributors will offer to help leaders when they get behind with their work, and they will share information that will help leaders achieve success.

The most successful two-way teamwork happens when leaders and contributors together set goals and develop action plans to achieve them. After setting the goals, leader and contributors together identify individual roles and responsibilities. They hold a team meeting once a week to coordinate team activities, check progress, and solve any problems that have arisen.

Two Ways About It

The leaders of one high-tech company approached me with a problem. Their employees constantly argued and fought with their co-workers and managers. Could I do anything about it?

I visited the workplace, wandered around, talked to people, and took notes everywhere I went. I discovered that the employees were under considerable stress from a number of factors: external competition, frequent changes in work methods and schedules, a feeling of having no control over their fate, their lives and their futures in the hands of others.

I helped the organization implement shared-management teams in which the employees had decision-making power for some of the changes that had to be made. The conflicts and arguments disappeared, and the contributors got excited about setting new performance records.

The basic problem at the company was stressed-out workers. Stuck in a situation where their opinions were not valued and where they had no voice in decisions, they reacted as most people do when surrounded by change, uncertainty, and lack of control — they lashed out at fellow workers and bosses.

Shared-management teams gave the employees some of the power they needed to take control of their lives. Participating in decision making gives contributors a sense that they are in charge of their future — a situation that dramatically reduces stress. Research shows that workers who have decision-making authority are less prone to stress-related illnesses.[3] Brain chemistry is healthier with two-way leadership.

The Side by Side Leadership Continuum (opposite) shows top-down behaviors at the negative (left) end of the continuum and two-way, Side by Side behaviors at the positive end. This scale is useful in rating where your organization's demonstrated leadership falls in relation to the worst and the best. Most leaders, of course, operate somewhere between the extremes. In the company with the employee problems, leadership fell somewhere on the negative side of center.

Do your leaders dominate discussions during meetings, do all the talking in one-on-one interactions, and refuse to listen to the ideas of others? It's obvious that their leadership belongs near the negative end of the spectrum. When leaders engage in any one of the three major top-down behaviors (dominating, authoritarian, or competitive), the other two top-down behaviors seem to follow automatically. Domineering behavior causes contributors to react emotionally, rather than rationally, and reduces their ability to think clearly and effectively about their work.

Two-way behavior in communication, power sharing, and teamwork locates the leader near the positive end. This is where you want to be as a leader, and it is where you

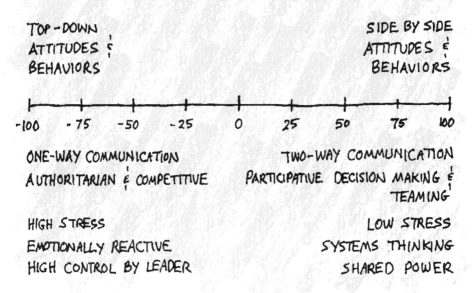

SIDE BY SIDE LEADERSHIP CONTINUUM

TOP-DOWN
ATTITUDES &
BEHAVIORS

SIDE BY SIDE
ATTITUDES &
BEHAVIORS

-100   -75   -50   -25   0   25   50   75   100

ONE-WAY COMMUNICATION
AUTHORITARIAN & COMPETITIVE

TWO-WAY COMMUNICATION
PARTICIPATIVE DECISION MAKING &
TEAMING

HIGH STRESS
EMOTIONALLY REACTIVE
HIGH CONTROL BY LEADER

LOW STRESS
SYSTEMS THINKING
SHARED POWER

want all your people to be in their leadership behavior. The quickest way to establish Side by Side Leadership is to encourage leaders to listen instead of talk. When leaders listen to their contributors, they are more apt to involve them in decision making, because they become more aware that contributors, too, have knowledge and good ideas. Over time, Side by Side Leadership creates the interactions that result in systematic thinking, creative solutions, and superior results.

Side by Side Tips

Here's what you should remember about Side by Side Leadership's two-way street:

- The most effective leadership arises from a two-way exchange of information, ideas, and cooperation.

- Side by Side leaders lead by listening, not talking.

- Decision-making authority should be shared, but a Side by Side leader can determine the level of sharing, depending on the type of decision involved.

- Engaging in two-way behaviors stimulates Side by Side Leadership patterns.

Chapter 6

Principle 2:

Interaction Fields

Bridging Resources across Internal and External Interaction Fields Grows New Assets

An interaction field is a set of relationships involving a group of leaders and contributors who mutually influence each other. Interaction fields exist both inside and outside organizations. Collectively, they form the system within which the leader influences and is influenced.

Looking at the diagrams we've used so far in this book, you may be wondering: Why is there a dashed line around each interaction? Here's why: An interaction field is the space inside the dashed line. Each type of relationship, each unit within an organization, has an interaction field: a one-on-one interaction, a team, a department, even the organization as a whole. The organization interacts with other

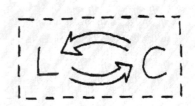

entities within the society's interaction field; a society interacts with other societies and its own environment within the physical world's interaction field.

The most basic interaction, one-on-one, is the leader-contributor interaction we introduced in chapter 2. See the dashed line around the leader and contributor? The line is dashed to represent the fact that the boundary around the interaction field is open — that is, the interaction field can influence and be influenced by people, groups, units, and forces outside itself. This type of relationship modeling is known as the Open Systems Model.

The Open Systems Model is analogous to certain physical laws. The Second Law of Thermodynamics states that energy systems move toward entropy — that is, toward disorder. Ilya Prigogene and other physicists noted that this law was not consistent with observations of cosmic evolution. His reconciliation, which is called the Theory of Dissipative Systems Inside Chaos Theory, states that although closed systems move toward entropy and destruction, open systems continue to evolve and develop.

Prigogene's theory applies to Side by Side Leadership as well. Leaders who open their interaction fields will be able to grow their businesses and continue to create wealth and abundance. That's what our dashed lines are meant to communicate.

Leaders operate inside interaction fields that exist inside other organizational interaction fields — like Russian matryoshka dolls, where each doll nests inside another, larger doll. Every organizational interaction field is influenced by the values, goals, and priorities of the organizational leaders, as well as the values, goals, and priorities of organizational stakeholders. The most effective team leaders are those who link the team to the organization's goals and to the other areas of the organization. The most effective knowledge leaders have strong ties outside their work group to other parts of the organization and to other organizations' knowledge leaders. They use these ties to further their organization's growth and success. These leaders are also adept at linking their knowledge work to the organization's visionary goals.

Many contributors are promoted rapidly to leadership positions that are beyond their experience because they grasp the bigger purpose of their organization and see the idealistic vision toward which it is pointed. These contributors

> Leaders who open their interaction fields will be able to grow their businesses and continue to create wealth.

and leaders not only do their jobs, they do them in ways that achieve organizational goals.

The top team leaders pay attention not only to the performance of their team and team members, but also to the values, goals, and priorities of the department and organization interaction fields in which the team functions.

External Interaction Fields

One of the most important truths about human behavior comes from the field of biology. Human beings, like all life forms, must adapt to changes in their physical environment in order to survive. Organizations work on the same principle: they must adapt to changes in their physical, social, and economic environment.[1] Companies like Studebaker and Philco no longer exist because they did not successfully adapt to changes in their business and society interaction fields.

Organizations depend on their leaders to identify what organizational changes must be made in response to threats and opportunities in the business environment. One of the classic textbooks for organizational leaders, Chester Barnard's *Function of the Executive*, states that the primary responsibility of an executive is to manage the relationship of the organization with the rest of the world.[2]

At one point in my career, I had a boss who was the top executive of a fairly successful 4,000-person organization. He spent much of his time away from his office, visiting board members, customers, and leaders of other organizations. I wondered why he devoted so much time to people outside the organization, and why, upon his return, he directed the other managers and me to make so many changes.

It was only later that I understood this principle: that a leader must understand and successfully relate his goals and work not only to his own interaction field but to adjacent and related fields as well. A good organizational leader maintains relationships with important external constituencies; he brings in new people with expertise; he encourages contributors to share these responsibilities. He knows that

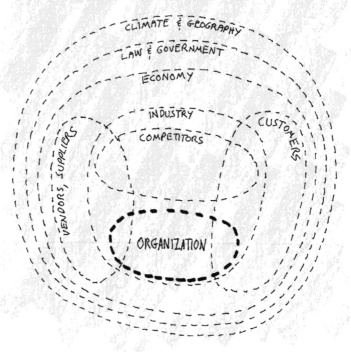

EXTERNAL INTERACTION FIELDS FOR A TYPICAL ORGANIZATION

CLIMATE & GEOGRAPHY

LAW & GOVERNMENT

ECONOMY

INDUSTRY

COMPETITORS

CUSTOMERS

VENDORS, SUPPLIERS

ORGANIZATION

these external relationships are essential for bringing new ideas and knowledge to the organization.

In the late 1990s, many leaders accelerated the growth of their organizations through joint ventures with customers, suppliers, even competitors. With oil and gas discoveries declining in North America, major oil companies formed joint ventures with drilling companies that had experience in the deep waters of the Gulf of Mexico. A single successful joint venture could put a traditional oil company in the deepwater drilling business.

In the first half of the twentieth century, Alfred P. Sloan used his expertise in creating external interaction fields to transform General Motors, a company on the verge of bankruptcy, into the largest enterprise in the world. Among other creative ideas, he formed an advisory council of car dealers that (1) provided ideas to GM's engineers for new car features and designs and (2) lobbied state and federal governments to build more highways; he sold GM cars at discount to high school driver's education programs, thus supporting road safety while establishing brand identification with new customers; and he sold fleets of discounted GM cars to government agencies, further establishing public brand identity. In addition to revitalizing General Motors, all of these interactions had a tremendous influence on American society's adoption of the automobile as part of its culture.

Do you know your own interaction fields? Use the next few minutes to find out. Draw an interaction field map of the major external influences on your organization: customers, suppliers, competitors, investors, industry, the industrial complex, government, society, and the physical environment.

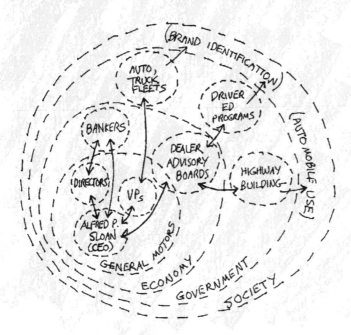

INTERACTION FIELDS OF GM CEO ALFRED P. SLOAN

Think of new types of relationships with these influences that might improve your organization's success.

Internal Interaction Fields

Leaders who create wealth and new resources engage and work in a variety of interaction fields. This is an important principle. Workers normally deal mostly with their "home" interaction field, the people they work with directly and see frequently. Side by Side leaders do, too, but they also interact with closely related fields in ways that can help their team and organization; they pay attention to their home interaction field and the next ring or two outward.

The influence of the contributor and the leader upon each other is one aspect of a Side by Side interaction field.

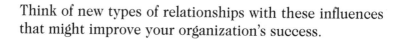

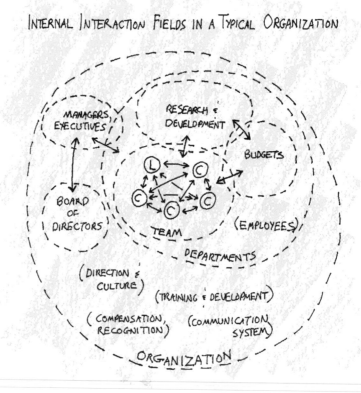

INTERNAL INTERACTION FIELDS IN A TYPICAL ORGANIZATION

All of the leader's and contributor's shared thoughts and actions happen inside this field — stated and unstated goals, expectations, attitudes, and problems. Both the leader and the contributor can influence the two-person interaction field in different ways to improve performance and results. They can improve their own values, thoughts, and behaviors; they can improve the quality of their shared interaction field; and they can share each other's functional knowledge and skills to achieve shared goals.

The power of Side by Side Leadership in a two-person interaction field multiplies the effectiveness of both leader and contributor. To project that effectiveness into organizational results, this two-person interaction must occur in an open field — that is, it must successfully influence and be influenced by a variety of team, work group, and departmental interaction fields, all of which exist in successive concentric rings within the organizational field. When the power of these two-way interactions is combined, the effect is to multiply the potential improvements. When the interactions are two-way instead of one-way, and when the goals of organizational leaders and contributors are aligned, the effective size of the organization increases exponentially.

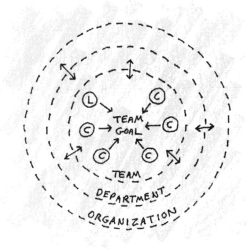

Many organizations find themselves afflicted by the "silo syndrome," with each department considering itself almost an independent entity rather than part of a larger organization. To cooperate with another silo is perceived as giving away vital resources. Side by Side leaders have found that one way to break the hold of this parochial attitude is to institute cross-functional teams that operate by engaging the skills and resources of other departments to reach a common goal.

Motorola increased the productivity of its pager manufacturing team by bringing in an engineer from the engineering department. To encourage communication with the pager assemblers, her desk was located near the manufacturing work floor. Together, the engineer and the assemblers came up with new ways to reduce assembly time. They tested the ideas, and those that worked were quickly adopted by everyone. Being close to the assembly team allowed the engineer to see readily what worked and what didn't; it also improved her relationship with the assemblers.

Leaders can create organizational interaction fields that draw innovative ideas for products and services from every employee. When they do, they should be ready to listen. General Electric CEO Jack Welch posed this challenge for leaders: "Create an environment where people can reach their dreams — and they don't have to do it in a garage."[3]

Mutual and Two-Way Interaction Fields

Two-person interaction fields exist within teams or work groups, teams within organizations, organizations within industries or governments, which exist within societies. All societies share the outermost interaction field — the natural world. Each of these fields interacts directly with adjacent fields and either directly or indirectly with all the other fields.

The interaction is usually two-way, whether by design or not. It is obvious that an organization can influence its work teams, but the converse is also true, and this influence is useful. A new idea that proves successful in a work team or a department can become a model for change in the entire organization. (Joel Barker, the futurist and innovation expert, has observed that the most successful innovations often originate in a department or team far from headquarters.[4]) This kind of trial by fire — the pilot program — is one of the fastest ways to bring about organizational change.

In the Side by Side Open Systems Model, this mutual influence between fields is essential to breaking down

---

YOUR SEARCH FOR INTERACTION BREAKTHROUGH

HERE ARE SOME THOUGHT-PROVOKING QUESTIONS ABOUT INTERACTION FIELDS THAT MIGHT HELP YOU IMPROVE YOUR RESULTS:

- WHAT ORGANIZATIONS OUTSIDE MY NORMAL INTERACTION FIELD COULD HELP MY ORGANIZATION ACHIEVE ITS VISIONARY GOALS?

- WHICH PEOPLE OUTSIDE MY ORGANIZATION COULD HELP MY ORGANIZATION ACHIEVE ITS VISIONARY GOALS?

- WHAT PEOPLE OR RESOURCES, IF I PARTNERED WITH THEM, WOULD HELP MY ORGANIZATION OR TEAM ACHIEVE BETTER RESULTS?

- IN WHAT WAYS COULD MY INTERNAL AND EXTERNAL CUSTOMERS BE CONSIDERED ALLIES WHO COULD HELP MY TEAM OR ORGANIZATION ACHIEVE ITS VISIONARY GOALS?

- WHAT PEOPLE OR ORGANIZATIONS OUTSIDE MY INTERACTION FIELD COULD BLOCK PROGRESS TOWARD MY GOALS? HOW CAN I TURN THEM INTO ALLIES?

I HOPE THAT AS YOU ANSWER THESE QUESTIONS YOU WILL DISCOVER NEW IDEAS AND POSSIBLE RELATIONSHIPS TO HELP YOU ACHIEVE YOUR TEAM AND ORGANIZATIONAL GOALS.

---

barriers to productivity, innovation, and timely adaptation to market changes. One of my customers wanted to transform his top-down organization into one that operated on the Side by Side model. Only 90 percent of the company's product output was meeting quality standards. His company had the silo problem, with leaders "protecting" their workers from "outside" distractions. We implemented team skills training that focused on a process — one that cut across four departments.

The departments were small, so it was natural to train four teams at once. As they learned and applied the team skills together, everyone recognized how important it was for the departments to share information promptly. They not only documented the process they used to manufacture the product, they also improved the way their work was planned and carried out. The silo dissolved, and work quality skyrocketed, with 99 percent of the product meeting the standard.

Interaction Field Resources

The five spheres of influence of Side by Side Leadership help leaders create and use resources from a variety of interaction fields. Personal, knowledge, and interpersonal influences facilitate success in any interaction field; team influence leads to successful interactions inside and outside organization teams; and organizational influence enables the leader to apply resources inside and outside the organization toward achieving organizational goals.

Side by Side Tips

Keep in mind the following principles of interaction fields:

- Side by Side Leadership is a system model with inside and outside individual, small group, and organizational interaction fields.

- Leaders who are open and two-way inside and across the different interaction fields achieve greater productivity than leaders who are one-way or closed.

- When leaders see and consider all the people and other resources in the different interaction fields, they are better able to deploy the resources to achieve their goals.

- Leaders can dramatically increase performance and create wealth when they use familiar resources in new ways, see new resources, and develop new combinations of new and familiar resources across interaction fields.

Chapter 7

Principle 3:

Visionary Goals

Shared Visionary Goals Magnetically Pull Innovative
Thinking and Increased Productivity

Not long ago, a group of oilfield
workers and their district supervisor were struggling to reduce their
production costs from $13 a barrel, which was almost the price of
oil at the time. The supervisor knew that unless those costs were
substantially reduced within six months, headquarters would close
the field and put everyone out of work. He immediately called a
meeting to explain the situation and discuss ways to reduce costs.

The Challenge of Survival

Using a method called structured brainstorming, the supervisor asked
workers to write down their ideas before the discussion began. He also
had them designate a few individuals as "wild idea" participants,
whose role was to think up some truly off-the-wall solutions.

It was one of these wild-idea contributors, the supervisor of a
warehouse full of parts and supplies, who came up with the largest
cost reduction. He suggested, and the group agreed, that they should
close his warehouse and draw on a similar one in operation nearby.
Prior to the team meeting, the group had resisted all efforts to close
their warehouse, even though the neighboring one contained the

same supplies. This and many other ideas they came up with cut costs enough to allow the workers to keep their jobs.

The real possibility that the company might have to close the oilfield and cut their jobs did more than force innovative thinking. It also pressed the workers to put their ideas into action as quickly as possible. As a result of their innovative thinking, costs dropped dramatically, from $13 per barrel to a phenomenal $3 per barrel.

The challenge of a direct threat to its existence can push an organization to find ways of surviving.

Work teams and wild animals know that one of the biggest incentives for high performance is the presence of a clear challenge to their survival. Authors John Katzenbach and Douglas Smith argued as much in *The Wisdom of Teams*.[1] I have found a similar factor at the organization level: when leaders accurately identify and clearly communicate the external threats to the organization's survival, all members of the organization are more responsive to new programs to improve the organization.

The challenge posed by a direct threat to its existence can push an organization, like a biological organism, to find ways of surviving. It focuses people's attention and clears the mind; unimportant issues fade away; innovation and breakthrough thinking suddenly come naturally.

But for a truly powerful effect on a company's fortunes, the push of danger can be coupled with the magnetic pull of specific, compelling goals. In a setting where communication, power, and teamwork are a shared experience, the combined effect of these incentives is a recipe for breakthrough performance. This is the case in Side by Side Leadership.

The Power of Specific Goals

University of Maryland psychologist Edwin Locke and colleagues across North America conducted ten hard-data studies of goal setting in a variety of businesses and work groups.[2] They found that productivity improved by 11 to 27 percent (on average, 16 percent) after leaders ensured that their work groups had

1. specific goals,

2. "reach-out" or "stretch" goals with high target levels, and

3. visible measures of goal results.

Locke discovered that a vague work goal, such as "Do your best," is not as effective as a specific goal for getting the best or the most work done. In one study, twenty logging crews were divided into two groups. Half of the crews were told to do their best, while the other half were given specific goals of how much timber to cut per day. The result? The logging crews with specific goals cut 92 percent more timber per week than the "do your best" crews. Based on what we already know about the effectiveness of shared goal setting, if you do nothing as a leader other than ensure that contributors have a hand in setting specific, reach-out goals and measuring the results, you will improve your team's performance.

Goals that are specific and that are set beyond past or current performance levels provide the necessary focus and direction for Side by Side Leadership relationships. In any interaction between a leader and team members, one question must be asked: How will the results of this interaction affect the achievement of our goals? The more specifically worded the goal, the easier it is for the leader to maintain the focus, especially within the complex team interaction field. Making shared goals clear and specific, and communicating them well, also eliminates the unhealthy conflict that often arises when team members interpret goals in different ways.

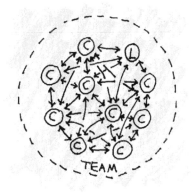

Wording goals in specific terms promotes intellectual focus; setting them high gives emotional focus. Some of the emotions, it is true, may be fear and anxiety, but these can motivate as well. Setting the bar high causes a shift in thinking to a more creative, resourceful mode: the old ways won't do it; what will? Once achieved, reach-out goals bring excitement, satisfaction, and self-confidence. Perhaps nothing is impossible after all.

One of my client companies had a group of engineers and drafting associates who had no specific goals; they just came to work and did as much drafting as they could each day. They were a bottleneck in the organization's process of getting new products designed, manufactured, and shipped.

We advised the company to begin setting specific goals. Once they did, the productivity of the group increased 34 percent — one-third more work — which quickly increased the company's profits.

The barrier to setting specific goals for teams and organizations is that individuals disagree on which specific goal is the right goal. Effective group facilitation can make the difference between vague, general goals and specific, measurable ones.

Shared Goal Setting

If setting specific, ambitious goals can produce such great results, a major leadership question still must be answered: Who should set the goals? It is now becoming clear, from a review of studies by Locke and Latham, that employees should definitely be involved when their knowledge is equal to or greater than their leader's.[3] Conversely, participation in goal setting by new or inexperienced employees is often not effective, because they may not have enough information to set realistic targets. You and I know this is true from personal experience; we may need to perform part of an unfamiliar task before we can reliably estimate a time for completion.

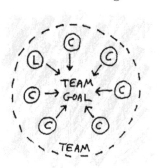

In another study, engineers performed better when they set their own quarterly improvement goals and tracked and reported their own progress.[4] This approach was clearly better than when the manager measured progress, and better than the current, widely popular "360-degree" peer-and-supervisor performance feedback approach.

Shared goal setting proved superior in still other studies. In one comparison study, one leader facilitated weekly meetings to set goals while another simply discussed the previous week's performance. Factory teams that set their own goals experienced 10 percent greater productivity, office workers almost 25 percent; the comparison group had only a 5 percent gain.[5] Four other studies of shared goal setting showed 20 to 70 percent performance gains.[6]

The Positive Spillover Effect

The beneficial effects of shared goal setting sometimes show themselves in unexpected ways. In one provocative study, a pizza delivery chain sought to reduce the accident rate of its drivers by improving their compliance with stop signs and traffic signals.[7]

At the beginning of the experiment, researchers secretly observed drivers' behavior at three intersections. Then the 324 drivers were divided into two study groups. In the first group, drivers participated in a one-hour discussion of the importance of coming to a complete stop, after which they were told that observers saw them doing so only 55 percent of the time. They were then asked to set their own goal: what percentage compliance should they aim for? They set a target of 75 percent. The second group was simply assigned a goal by the manager: 75 percent compliance.

The results were surprising. Both groups improved equally in complying with stop signs and traffic lights. There was no apparent advantage to inviting employee participation. But researchers were startled to discover that the drivers who set their own goals went further: they improved in two other areas. They used their turn signals and their seat belts more often — two safety measures that were not even discussed. This powerful "positive spillover" effect resulted in overall safer driving.

During structured team-skills training that my firm was conducting at his company, another supervisor was surprised by the positive spillover effect. His manufacturing team had participated in setting quality improvement goals, but even before the team had begun to work toward those goals, its overall productivity rose sharply — an improvement that had not been addressed. How was this possible? I told him it often happened that when goal setting was shared with team members in one area of work, there was "positive spillover" to performance improvement in a different area. Contributors whose ideas and opinions are respected are more likely to improve their performance spontaneously in other areas. It's a matter of ownership and self-confidence.

Setting Visionary Goals

Another of my oil industry clients, Vastar Resources, needed outside help to climb out of a slump. Its production was growing by only 4 percent per year, which put it below average in its class in a very competitive industry. The executives' first attempt was to formulate a "new vision" for the company: to "be the best" in its field. The organization reacted with a giant yawn.

Since the first attempt had failed to stimulate innovative thinking, Vastar agreed to try our recommendation of setting a truly visionary goal. The new goal would be to triple annual performance. The response this time was "Wow!" People complained, asked questions, insisted it couldn't be done. But one thing was certain: it generated excitement.

Everyone realized it would take breakthrough thinking to triple the company's performance. Every work team saw itself as a key player and revised its goals to meet the challenge of the company goal. On their own, people began proposing innovative strategies, finding creative solutions to problems, and designing inventive work plans for achieving the goal. They took great risks; they knew that to achieve the visionary goal, every work process would have to be radically improved. "Business as usual" went out the window; such a performance improvement could not be achieved with status quo thinking.

Within three years, Vastar's increase in performance and total shareholder return put it at the top of its group of independent, large-capitalization oil and gas companies. The challenge of achieving "impossible" but visionary goals was what put it there — that, and harnessing the talents and skills of all its contributors through Side by Side Leadership.

Visionary goals must conform to this general principle: each must have a clear and measurable target that describes the desired end result. The leader, of course, sets the visionary goals side by side with contributors, brainstorming and selecting the goals together. The goals are called "visionary" because they describe a very specific vision: a highly desirable, almost idealistic result that will be accomplished by a particular time in the future. Research shows that setting such goals brings about great improvements in, among other things, work processes, because setting goals stimulates people to develop and share creative ideas for achieving them.[8]

The way the work is done must change if we are to reach visionary goals.

Visionary goals state specifically what is desired by the leaders and the members of the organization, their teams, their city, their country, or their families. Visionary goals go well beyond the expected. They elicit the response, "Wow! Can we achieve that?" when first unveiled. Indeed, they *cannot* be reached doing things the way they have always been done. The way the work is done *must change* if we are to reach visionary goals.

The Push-Pull Effect

The combination of a push from a threat to survival and a pull from a visionary goal (see next page) is a powerful stimulant for change and progress. Companies that use this stimulant to best effect, that engage through Side by Side Leadership the full range of employee skills, talents, knowledge, and commitment, stand the best chance of achieving dramatic outcomes.

Side by Side Tips

Here are the important points to remember about formulating and achieving shared visionary goals:

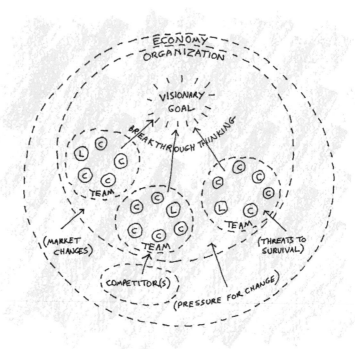

- If you want breakthrough thinking and results, set visionary goals side by side.

- Threats to the survival of an organization, if accurately identified and communicated to the members, can push that organization to achieve its goals.

- Visionary goals pull an entire organization toward success.

- Clear visionary goals with the "Wow!" factor instill the need for creative thinking and doing the right things in different, better ways.

- Shared goal setting significantly improves performance.

- When a leader facilitates Side by Side goal setting with contributors in one area of performance, there will be "positive spillover" — improvements in other areas of work as well.

Chapter 8

Principle 4:

Focused Creativity

Fostering Outside-the-Box Thinking Produces Breakthrough Ideas

Advanced Micro Devices' Submicron Development Center in Sunnyvale, California, wanted to help manufacture and produce AMD's newest computer chip. Jim Doran, the center's leader, knew that if he could reconfigure his team for high-volume production, they could make a ton of money for the company.

Unfortunately, the changeover was not going smoothly. The first six months of the project brought one technical challenge after another. Jim brought key staff members together to review the problems; they acknowledged that the center would come nowhere near their year-end goal.

This was the kind of situation that would have caused many supervisors to yell and assign blame. But Jim didn't blow up. Instead, he remained calm — and led staff members in a little structured brainstorming.

"Imagine," he said, "that it's New Year's Eve. We've finished the project. We've solved all the big problems, made up for lost time, and met our production goals.

"Now, I want each of you to write down on a piece of paper exactly what happened this year that allowed us to meet our goal."

The process was like climbing a steep mountain and then looking back to see what had been accomplished. After they finished writing, the staff members shared their ideas with each other, one idea at a time. The meeting room became charged with excitement; people began to see, hear, and feel the options and possibilities. Not long after that meeting, they put together a creative strategy.

Leaders who lead side by side establish a work and interaction climate that promotes creative thinking at all levels.

From that point forward, the goal began to look achievable. There were more meetings, more bad news, and more technical challenges, but Jim calmly probed for the facts and prodded the team for creative solutions — sometimes practical, sometimes wild and off-the-wall. He got them to do their best thinking, encouraging openness, creativity, and risk-taking. At the same time, to stimulate creative thinking at all levels of the organization, he began team leadership training for all employees.

Jim and his management team, to their chagrin, also learned that they were part of the problem — a bottleneck for more than 500 decisions, they were told. To solve this problem, they delegated most of their decision making and turned their full attention to the most creative recommendations. Instead of a bottleneck, they became a conduit for breakthrough ideas that ended up netting the company almost a half billion dollars in extra profit.

Leaders who lead side by side, like Jim Doran, establish a work and interaction climate that promotes creative thinking at all levels. Hundreds of small creative improvements day by day, task by task, add up to big improvements overall — especially on the bottom line.

A Package Deal

I was talking with the new president of a company with revenues of $100 million a year; the topic was visionary goals. "Dennis," he said, "I do not believe in setting reach-out goals that are impossible to meet. I've worked for bosses who did that, and it doesn't work."

He was right. Most leaders seek those fantastic 30 to 300 percent performance improvements they read about

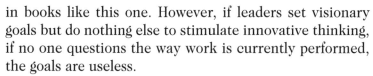
in books like this one. However, if leaders set visionary goals but do nothing else to stimulate innovative thinking, if no one questions the way work is currently performed, the goals are useless.

Breakthrough results don't come with everybody simply typing faster, walking faster, or lifting more; people can't work at 100 percent week after week, year after year. Breakthrough results require breakthrough thinking — everyone working smarter and thinking creatively.

Creative thinking achieves visionary goals by allowing team members to look at resources in new ways and transform them into new products or services. The most creative of them can even transform mistakes or problems into success stories. The founders of the Minnesota Mining and Manufacturing Company (3M) took a problem — a mine full of low-grade corundum — and turned it into a wide range of commercially successful sandpaper products. The tradition lives on; one 3M engineer took a "failed" adhesive experiment and turned it into a world-beating office product: Post-it® notes.

Principles of Innovative Thinking

Creativity research has shown us ways to transform memo writers into innovative thinkers. These activities are useful with teams and groups:

- Generate as many ideas as possible by setting a numerical goal: "Let's come up with fifty ideas — good, bad, sane, or crazy — in the next ten minutes."

- List all ideas offered, regardless of how practical or "good" they are.

- Develop imaginative ideas by introducing random words to stimulate ideas, however unlikely the connection. Words that conjure up images of real objects ("zipper," "fire," "airplane") or actions ("skiing," "growing," "dancing") are especially useful for breaking through the thought barrier that surrounds a problem. (This technique was championed by British creativity researcher Edward DeBono, who held that any activity that jars one out of ordinary thinking stimulates creative thinking.)

I was once brainstorming ideas with a management group that had a problem with "Jack," the manager of another group. The group I was working with had asked Jack to implement new services they knew their customers desired. Jack had turned them down. They were angry at Jack's resistance to the new ideas; they thought he was just being mean and petty, using his power just to thwart them.

We spent about three minutes individually writing down ideas on sticky notes. Then I introduced a new word: "Ice." I asked everyone to write down any ideas related to the word "ice," no matter how wild, for getting Jack's support.

Next, I asked them to read aloud their ideas, one at a time. As they did, I placed their sticky notes on a white flip chart for everyone to see. First came the pre-"ice" solutions:

● Make a formal presentation to Jack.

● Make a formal presentation to Jack's boss.

● Gather data to support the new service proposal.

Then we got into the "wild" ideas. "Send Jack to the North Pole," said one participant. The team snickered. "Ice Jack," said someone else. This got a big laugh.

Then someone said, "Let's take Jack out and buy him a Scotch on the rocks."

There were other ideas, both ordinary and wild, but by the end of the brainstorming session, the group had settled on two ideas. The first was a spinoff of the "Scotch on the rocks" idea: they took Jack out to dinner, got better acquainted with him as a person, and asked him to share his vision and goals for the organization. The other thing they did was compile data supporting their idea for new services and present it to Jack to "melt" his objections.

The two-pronged strategy worked. Jack "thawed." He approved a pilot program. He also became an advocate for more of the group's ideas — largely because they had taken the time to hear his vision and goals. The team's use of Side by Side Leadership and structured creativity turned a problem into an asset.

Creative thinking is not just for the company's research and development department. Every part of the organization can be innovative. The eight members of a Raytheon Montek metals processing team in Salt Lake City demonstrated innovative thinking. Their work, metal-plating the aircraft parts their company manufactured, contaminated the water used in the process. To comply with environmental regulations, they had to pay for costly water treatment. After some creative-thinking training, the team decided to treat the water in-house and recover the waste metal for resale — an innovation that saved the company a lot of money.

Incubating Premature Ideas

When people brainstorm alone or in groups, they often come up with wild ideas that are not fully developed. The leader can either throw these ideas away, or she can "incubate" them, much like premature babies, nurturing them into healthy, useful lives.

Mihaly Csikszentmihalyi (pronounced "CHICK-sent-me-high-ee") studied the most creative individuals of the twentieth century. In his book *Creativity,* he showed that although Nobel Prize winners and other innovative leaders were very diverse in their thinking, all agreed on the importance of incubating ideas: "Let problems simmer below the threshold of consciousness for a time."[1] Shakespeare was said to have been idle between plays. Donald Campbell, a highly creative psychologist and scientist, left the car radio off while driving to increase his incubation time. Walking, hiking, jogging, and swimming are other ways leaders found valuable incubation time for creative ideas.

Incubating wild, undeveloped ideas means revisiting them, adding information, trying them out, pruning them, and bouncing them off others. Properly cared for, wild seedling ideas can grow into innovations that lead the way into the future. Without planned incubation, wild ideas wither and die; their potential is lost; organizations suffer.

When Leaders Get Innovative

Getting out of the daily routine promotes innovation. Citicorp CEO John Reed composed his most creative business plans at the beach or on a park bench. Redesigning workers' jobs to be less routine and boring has raised productivity, particularly in companies where workers trained in teamwork skills were involved in redesigning their own jobs to make the work more meaningful.[2]

The highest form of innovative thinking is to combine the truths from two opposite points of view. Tolerating ambiguity, even nurturing the two opposites, allows for the eventual synthesis of the best of both. The trick is being able to handle the mental tension between opposing ideas. Albert Einstein practiced this type of thinking in formulating his theories of relativity. Dr. Murray Bowen, the originator of family systems theory, stimulated his creative thinking by considering the most extreme viewpoint. A study by Judith Kolb found that the most successful leaders were those who tolerated uncertainty, letting ideas simmer on the back burner, instead of jumping to quick solutions; they consciously exercised their minds to prevent their thinking from falling into predictable patterns.[3]

Work Smarter, Work Better

Learning and applying innovative thinking improves work performance in both leaders and contributors. Workers in every job want to feel that their daily job is a work of art, a real contribution. Whether it's creating a sales plan, responding to a customer's request, or assembling a computer, workers achieve the greatest satisfaction when they are allowed to be creative, to try out new ideas, to continuously improve the way they do their work.

One team of software programmers that I trained developed a forty-step project action plan that would take six months to complete. Unfortunately, they were given only two months to do it. So they got creative. They eliminated steps, combined and sequenced tasks, found previously developed code they could use. Enthusiasm grew; team members who had not been very active volunteered for major tasks. Even the team leader's manager, who had stayed on the sidelines, found ways to help. Applying small, creative solutions, the team completed the work in two months.

> The best, most innovative ideas find a whole new way of viewing a problem.

Incremental creative improvements are valuable, because they can add up to total improvements of 10 to 20 percent. But what if your business needs to improve by 100 percent? Is there a model of creative thinking that can stimulate such a breakthrough improvement? Yes, there is.

Futurist/innovation expert Joel Barker discovered that people in all organizations think about their enterprise, its current products and services and customers, in certain mental patterns or frameworks that he calls "paradigms."[4] Barker found that he could train business leaders to list their current patterns or business assumptions, then to challenge those assumptions and come up with new paradigms.

One of his best examples is how Seiko and Texas Instruments undercut Swiss watchmakers with a new paradigm for a watch. Even though the Swiss originally conceived of the idea of a digital quartz watch, they were blocked from seeing its widespread potential by their old paradigm: a watch was a mechanical thing, driven by a spring.

The best, most innovative ideas find a whole new way of viewing a problem. The latest innovation in bulletproof glass was such a paradigm-breaking idea. Did bullets have to bounce off? Not necessarily, it seemed. The result? A new glass material that would give like a net and catch the bullet.

Side by Side Tips

A leader who leads side by side creates a climate of work and interaction that promotes creative thinking. Here are several ways Side by Side leaders can promote and use the best thinking of everyone in the organization:

- Stimulate innovative thinking to achieve break-through results.

- Seek large numbers of ideas by setting goals; record them all, even the most impractical.

- Use random visual words to stimulate imaginative ideas, no matter how crazy the connection.

- Incubate undeveloped ideas to full maturity.

- Formally train and encourage innovative thinking.

Chapter 9

Principle 5:

Structured Participation

Facilitating Total Participation Arouses Extraordinary Commitment

Side by Side leaders often bring key people together to brainstorm innovative ideas for achieving breakthrough. The key to getting everyone's best thinking is to use structured participation methods to facilitate the creative thinking of all, not just the vocal few.

Research summarized by Gryskiewicz found that groups with one highly vocal group member (or leader) were characterized by excessively uniform thinking.[1] This result is often called "group-think," and it is one of the main arguments used by critics to attack the use of teams in the workplace.

But "groupthink" is not true group thinking at all; it is just a shallow, one-dimensional examination of an issue dominated by one or two individuals. For true brainstorming to occur, the leader must make sure every member of the group gets to participate in

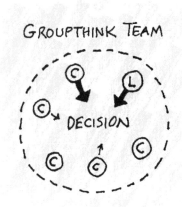

GROUPTHINK TEAM

the discussion and decision making. When one person dominates, other minds check out.

Unstructured "brainstorming" can have disastrous results. In one aerospace company, the president assembled his fifteen top managers and asked for their ideas on how to reverse the company's financial slide. He had good reason; they were losing money month after month, and his job was in jeopardy.

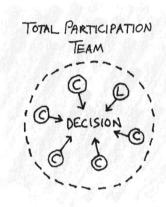

TOTAL PARTICIPATION
TEAM
DECISION

One person immediately hollered, "Don't send memos to everyone!"

"Cut travel costs!" came another voice.

Others joined in the chorus: "Cut every department's budget by 20 percent!" "Eliminate training and the training staff!"

"Eliminate half the research and development staff," said a manufacturing manager. This brought an immediate retort from the vice president of R&D: "Fire all those high-priced middle managers and engineers in manufacturing." The meeting quickly devolved into a twenty-minute shouting match between these two managers.

Finally, the leader interrupted. "Here's what we'll do," he told them. "We'll cut costs 15 percent across the board. Fifteen percent out of everyone's budget. And we'll cut travel and copying costs."

Three months later, the company's financial situation was no better, and the leader was fired. It was obvious that something other than cost cutting was needed, but the groupthink that came out of the unstructured brainstorming had everyone blindly chasing the first shouted idea. It also caused conflict, as each manager sought to cut costs in other managers' areas.

Two years later, the company finally began to get it right. They focused their marketing efforts in areas of proven strength. They started collecting a two-year backlog of accounts receivable — an amount that equaled one year's total operating expenses. These ideas could easily have been discovered in the first meeting if the leader had imposed a structured brainstorming approach to promote individual thinking.

Why Some People Hate Brainstorming

The example above, a true story, illustrates the typical, unstructured approach to brainstorming. It shows why most leaders cringe when they hear the "B" word. Especially engineers; many of them hate all meetings but reserve particular scorn for brainstorming sessions. "Leave me out of it. Let me stay in my cubicle and brainstorm the problem by myself. I'll come up with better solutions."

You know what? They're right. Research shows that people who brainstorm alone produce more and better ideas than people who brainstorm in an unstructured group.[2]

But wait. There's more research. Groups that use structured brainstorming outperform both unstructured groups and individuals brainstorming alone.[3] In fact, when leaders facilitated groups using structured brainstorming methods, the groups produced three times as many ideas as regular brainstorming groups.

> Groups using structured brainstorming methods produced three times as many ideas as regular brainstorming groups.

Imagine First, Discuss Later

A key step in structured brainstorming is the first one. As soon as the topic is introduced, participants are asked to write down their ideas without discussing them. This step alone doubles the number of creative or novel ideas, as well as ideas that prove more useful in the long run.[4]

Writing down as many ideas as possible before beginning the discussion stimulates divergent thinking. In the story above, when the first manager suggested reducing copying costs, it pulled everyone into thinking solely about cost cutting before anyone else had a chance to open up another line of discussion. This limited the scope of ideas.

Divergent creative thinking generates more and better ideas. Think of it in terms of a group of people lost, with only a compass to guide them. In unstructured brainstorming, the first person to speak says the way out lies to the south, because of fact X. Everybody else thinks of other reasons to go south: fact Y, fact Z, and so on. If everybody were instructed to write down their ideas before anyone spoke, several good reasons to go east, west, or north might be discovered and developed, and the best course might turn out to be some other direction entirely.

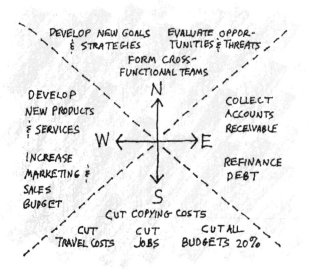

The more ideas at the start, the better. Under pressure, humans tend to revert to one of two instinctive reactions: fight or flight. Writing down ideas rather than throwing them immediately to the mercy of other participants reduces stress on thinkers, especially those whose ideas are so innovative they scare even the innovator. Rather than two alternative directions, the structured group may end up with more like six. Any organization that can triple its creativity will have a great advantage over its competitors.

Another step that boosts creativity is to ask participants to write down a specific number of ideas: say, a minimum of five. Just as with setting a specific goal ("The Power of Specific Goals," chapter 7), this simple request produces more ideas than "as many as you can think of."[5]

Structured creativity methods work best when one person, the meeting facilitator, leads the discussion and provides instructions. Teams with a trained facilitator have been shown to produce 45 percent more ideas than teams without.[6]

One of the facilitator's roles is to encourage and promote positive thinking and restrict negative criticism until all ideas have been presented. Criticizing or explaining ideas as they are being generated is like uprooting a plant that has just emerged above the surface of the soil. A seedling can be transplanted more successfully after it has matured a little. Structured brainstorming avoids early criticism of creative ideas, helping groups produce many more of them.

Good Leaders Go Last

A leader who facilitates a group should also contribute ideas, but not before all others have had a turn. In a study of nineteen teams formed to solve work-related problems, leaders in half of the groups were required to wait and listen to other members' ideas before presenting their own; in the other groups, leaders introduced the problem and then immediately presented their own solutions. Teams whose leaders spoke last produced 17 percent more solutions, and more feasible solutions, than teams whose leaders presented their own ideas first.[7]

The teams whose leaders solicited others' ideas first were also more likely to implement the solutions they created. The same principle is at work here as in a simple two-person leader-contributor interaction (chapter 2), which showed a 15 percent jump in productivity when the contributor spoke first. A leader who waits until last is in a better position to help consolidate the ideas presented into an objective consensus.

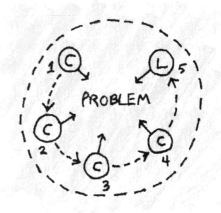

Any leader or contributor can use structured brainstorming to facilitate total group participation. The marketing manager of a high-tech company facilitated a structured brainstorming session with his product-line engineers. Using visual words to stimulate imaginative thinking, he asked team members to identify at least seven new products, or new applications for existing products, and to write

KEY STEPS OF STRUCTURED BRAINSTORMING

TO PROMOTE PARTICIPATION BY EVERYONE, THE LEADER OR OTHER TEAM MEMBER SHOULD FACILITATE THE GROUP BY DOING THE FOLLOWING:

1. CLEARLY, BUT CONCISELY, COMMUNICATE THE TOPIC TO BE BRAINSTORMED.

2. TELL ALL PARTICIPANTS TO WRITE DOWN AT LEAST FIVE OF THEIR OWN IDEAS, INCLUDING ONE "WILD" IDEA.

3. AFTER EVERYONE HAS WRITTEN FIVE IDEAS, INTRODUCE A RANDOM VISUAL WORD, LIKE "ICE" OR "FLYING," AND ASK PARTICIPANTS TO COME UP WITH A RELATED IDEA.

4. HAVE EACH PERSON, IN TURN, CONTRIBUTE ONE IDEA AT A TIME, WITH NO DISCUSSION OR CRITICISM, LEADER GOING LAST EACH TURN, UNTIL ALL IDEAS ARE PRESENTED. WRITE OR POST EACH WRITTEN IDEA WHERE ALL CAN SEE IT.

5. ENTERTAIN SUPPORTIVE COMMENTS FOR EACH PERSON'S IDEAS.

6. AFTER ALL IDEAS ARE DISPLAYED, HAVE PARTICIPANTS WORK OUT PRACTICAL WAYS TO USE THE WILD IDEAS.

7. HAVE THE TEAM SELECT IDEAS FOR IMMEDIATE USE, AND PUT FEASIBLE WILD IDEAS INTO THE INCUBATOR FOR FURTHER STUDY.

them down before discussing them. Three years later, this manager told me they were still using that list of ideas, and that one of the ideas had generated $250 million in additional revenue. What's more, he said, the product engineers, who had been competitive to the point of antagonism, had begun working together and had designed and moved several new products to market in one-fourth the usual time.

Shake It Up

Using the same structured brainstorming steps in the same order, time after time, can end up feeling repetitive and inhibit creative thinking. Avoid going stale by varying the routine: meet at different times, in different places; pass around a *Dilbert* cartoon; start the meeting with five minutes of tai chi. Laughter stimulates creativity; tell a joke. Get people to brainstorm before the meeting; collect the ideas when they meet. Brainstorm in subgroups and have them present their best ideas to the full group. Rotate the facilitating duties, or bring in outside facilitators. Instead of using sticky notes, write down ideas using colored markers on a flip chart. The only firm rule should be to stay true to the research-based principles.

AMD exec Jim Doran (chapter 8) often engaged participants in his management meetings by choosing one important agenda item and asking team members to write down their thoughts about it. He then asked each to read his notes aloud. Not only was this excellent Side by Side Leadership, it usually generated a variety of creative ideas that would not have occurred to him.

As president of a joint Texas Instruments–Samsung factory in Portugal, Jose Morais hired two outside facilitators to help develop creative business strategies for a failing organization. They invited creative thinkers from all levels of the organization to meetings with management staff to help brainstorm strategies for reaching their visionary goals. After implementing the creative strategies, the plant became one of the best manufacturing facilities in the world and won Portugal's National Quality Award.

THE SAME RESEARCH-BASED STEPS THAT GUIDE STRUCTURED BRAINSTORMING CAN HELP LEADERS FACILITATE PROBLEM SOLVING, DECISION MAKING, AND OTHER MANAGEMENT PROCESSES USING STRUCTURED PARTICIPATION METHODS. FOR EXAMPLE, IN A PROBLEM-SOLVING SESSION:

1. SPECIFY THE PROBLEM.

2. IDENTIFY THE CAUSES.

3. BRAINSTORM SOLUTIONS THAT ADDRESS THE CAUSES.

4. CONDUCT A PRO/CON ANALYSIS OF THE MAJOR SOLUTIONS TO SELECT THE BEST ONE.

5. DEVELOP THE GOAL AND METHODS FOR MEASURING PROGRESS TOWARD ACHIEVING IT.

6. DEVELOP AN ACTION PLAN, IMPLEMENT THE PLAN, AND MEASURE THE RESULTS.

Structured for Success

Mike Greig, an engineering leader at AMD's computer chip factory in Austin, told me that engineers often came to problem-solving meetings upset because of engineering problems that were costing the company thousands of dollars. They were not in a breakthrough-thinking frame of mind, so Mike would begin a meeting by following the structured problem-solving process by the book. Gradually the thinking would shift from emotionally reactive to calm and creative. Innovative problem solving by these engineering teams went on to boost the company's profits by hundreds of thousands of dollars.

Following the steps is important in getting the full benefit of structured brainstorming. The two most important steps are to (1) word the question or topic as specifically as possible, then (2) have participants individually write down their ideas before introducing them. Structuring the process, encouraging open dialogue, and practicing the principles of Side by Side Leadership will pay off in large numbers of creative solutions.

Side by Side Tips

Remember these key points about structured brainstorming:

- Using unstructured brainstorming can prove disastrous.

- A structured process tones down intense emotions in the workplace, allowing objective, creative thinking to emerge.

- In facilitating Side by Side Leadership, use structured brainstorming to get everyone's ideas.

- If you're the leader, present your own ideas last.

- Word the question or topic as specifically as possible, then have participants write down their ideas before presenting them.

- Vary your approach, but follow the principles.

Chapter 10

Principle 6:

Proven Knowledge

Filtering Creative Ideas through the Sieve of Knowledge and Experience Separates Out Workable Innovations

In his book *Creativity,* Mihaly Csikszentmihalyi (chapter 8) named Jacob Rabinow one of the eighty most creative individuals in the last half of the twentieth century.[1] Rabinow received 230 U.S. patents on a wide range of mechanical and electrical devices, including an automatic clock regulator that was used in all American autos, an automatic letter sorter that was adopted by the U.S. Post Office, the "best match" principle used in optical and magnetic character-reading machines, and the straight-line phonograph. Here's how Rabinow described the way he brainstormed and selected ideas to develop:

> You must think of a lot of music, a lot of ideas, a lot of poetry, a lot of whatever. And if you're good, you must be able to throw out the junk immediately without even saying it. In other words, you get many ideas appearing and you discard them because you're well trained and you say, "that's junk" . . . And that doesn't mean everyone can vote on it; they don't know enough.[2]

Rabinow knew the importance of knowledge and experience in winnowing out the best ideas. In selecting the most valuable ideas for their company, teams and their leaders depend on the same kind of expertise. Teams are great at brainstorming up a huge reservoir of innovative options, but it takes knowledgeable individuals to guide the team in picking the best alternatives.

Teams are great at brainstorming up innovative ideas but need knowledgeable individuals to help them pick the best options.

Psychologist Edwin Locke discovered that when leaders set specific, reach-out targets for simple work tasks, productivity dramatically increases. Complex work like planning a new factory or designing a new product cannot be performed effectively by simply setting the bar high and working hard. It requires selecting effective strategies based on the best available knowledge.[3]

Take, for example, an automobile glass factory Ford Motor Company built in the 1980s. After losing money on it for several years, Ford brought in an outside expert. The expert calculated the plant's highest ideal production capability — then proved that the plant could never show a profit because it had been designed too small. The plant had to be closed, with devastating consequences for everyone involved.

In one computer-chip company, engineers and operators tried out some some creative ideas to increase quality and productivity, but the effort failed. Their manager had, at their request, purchased special equipment, but it was constantly breaking down and could not be repaired. The problem? The manager had bought unreliable equipment from the lowest bidder. He did not have the knowledge or experience to understand that the best and most expensive equipment would have paid for itself within a month.

Taking Calculated Risks

Chaparral Steel is one of the world's most productive steelmakers. In the early 1990s, when the average cycle time to produce a rolled ton of steel in the United States, Japan, and Germany was 5.3, 5.6, and 5.7 employee-hours, respectively, Chaparral's average was an astounding 1.5. In achieving this productivity record, CEO Gordon Forward led the company in some calculated risk taking. Forward says, "We look at risk differently from other people. We always ask,

What is the risk of doing nothing? We don't bet the company, but if we're not taking some calculated risks, we stop growing, and we may die."[4]

Chaparral's leaders question planned improvement ideas, sometimes with an eye not to reducing risk but to increasing it: no risk, no breakthrough. According to Professor Dorothy Leonard of Harvard, they use risk taking to create new knowledge: "Chaparral managers avoid risk-less projects because a 'sure thing' holds no promise of competitive advantage, no opportunity to out-learn competitors."[5]

Chaparral made knowledge seeking part of its culture. When a major problem arose, representatives from different functions called a team meeting to discuss the issue. Team members then had forty-eight hours to get ideas and opinions from the world's top experts. After two days, they reconvened to share what they had learned and to apply the new information toward a solution.

The Risk of Thinking

Calculated risk taking can be divided into two parts: risk in thinking and risk in implementing the ideas. Taking risks in thinking is especially vital in cases of emotional crisis or a threat to the company's survival. This is when a leader must stay calm, uninhibit everyone's thinking, and encourage new ideas. The leader should create a safe, uncritical work environment and ask for wild ideas without regard to time, cost, custom, or practicality.

Meeting threats to survival or making major advances requires coming up with ideas that don't fit the pattern of other people's thoughts — that is, thinking "outside the box." It means looking for the possible in the seemingly impossible, seeing things in new ways, questioning assumptions, encouraging innovative thinking. All of these things carry the risk of failure. But not to take this risk carries a bigger risk — the near certainty that your company will fail or a more creative competitor will leave you behind.

True breakthrough thinking means considering the impossible. The people of Edison's time thought electric lights impossible. Alexander Graham Bell also did the impossible when he developed electric wires and a mechanical apparatus that allowed people to converse at a distance. The Wright brothers flew despite their naysayers.

Yet some leaders are afraid of creative thinking. They mistakenly assume that their workers will rush out of the brainstorming meeting and tear the company apart by irresponsibly implementing some of the wilder ideas. This just doesn't happen; it can't happen if a leader ensures that, before implementation, ideas are filtered through the sieve of knowledge and experience.

The Risk of Doing

When the time comes to take action, having as much information as possible reduces the risk by making it easier to predict the results accurately. Data should be collected and analyzed from as many sources as feasible, both inside and outside the organization. One company, needing to scale back the number of its product lines, used internal sales and profit data to help decide which to keep. But the marketing manager also collected outside data on customers' spending on competing products. Analysis of this information showed that the company's newest, highest-risk product had the potential to generate ten times more money than any other product.

Because the creative flow of ideas usually stops as soon as the critique begins, evaluation should occur either at the end of the primary brainstorming session or after. Once all the creative options are identified, teams and leaders should draw on the best knowledge available to evaluate innovative ideas and strategies.

An excellent way to compare ideas is a pro/con analysis, which usually leads to better decisions than an unstructured discussion. Together the leader and team members can apply their knowledge to the options to identify the positive and negative aspects of each. Which has the most benefits? Which has the fewest drawbacks? Sometimes the best option is clear. At other times, it becomes apparent that more information is needed; when this happens, the leader should recruit volunteers to obtain the missing knowledge.

General Electric found a way to get people thinking outside the box, but tempered the risk of implementing the ideas and saved millions of dollars as a result. In a process called "Work-out," employees were invited to a meeting in which, over several days, they were encouraged to help improve the company's policies and procedures by identifying wasteful practices and, in general, raising questions about the way everything was done. The employees surpassed expectations; they proposed totally eliminating some of the more restrictive policies and procedures. All recommendations were studied in the light of available knowledge and filtered through pro/con analysis before any changes were adopted.

Pilot Testing

Information is an essential ingredient in minimizing risk. Leaders and teams should, however, avoid "analysis paralysis" — the compulsion to keep collecting and analyzing data rather than making a decision. I've seen management teams, thinking the risks and costs too high, delay for months a decision to train work groups in structured team skills. Fortunately, there's an alternative to full and immediate implementation of breakthrough ideas: the pilot test.

Iowa State University communication professor Everett Rogers reviewed 4,000 studies on how risky innovations actually get put into action.[6] The best method, he found, was to try them out on a small scale. A pilot test can gauge the chances of success while minimizing the risk inherent in full-scale implementation. It yields real data on both the advantages and the disadvantages. It creates new knowledge for the leader, the team, and the organization.

Iowa State agriculture professors invented a new seed corn hybrid that grew taller and produced better yields; but how to get farmers to plant it? They cultivated small test plots on land near the farmers' fields. Farmers driving by could see for themselves how much taller and greener the hybrid plants grew and, when they grew curious and got out of their trucks for a closer inspection, how much healthier and more abundant the new plants and ears of corn looked.

One manager of an electric parts manufacturer was unsure about implementing structured team skills, so he selected one team for a pilot program. The team's productivity rose 20 percent within two months. Suddenly, all the managers wanted their teams trained.

Pharmaceutical manufacturers manage greater risks than most companies; their risk management practices are models for any leader. They conduct pilot trials consisting of rigorously controlled experiments, usually with outside or third-party oversight to avoid even unconscious bias. The companies adhere to the principle of pilot testing but surround the trials with experimental controls.

Despite the image conjured up by the word itself, a breakthrough is usually not a sudden, world-changing leap, but the sum of many small steps. Indeed, true creativity is often a series of tiny pilot tests. A study at the Chicago Art Institute comparing the most creative artists with those less inspired showed results that at first seem counter-intuitive: mediocre artists started out with a plan and stuck to it; the best artists made many false starts and tried many experiments in getting to their desired result.

Pilot experiments and small adjustments are a good way to avoid both overanalysis and big mistakes. Pilot studies promote breakthrough thinking by making it easier and less risky. You don't have to have all the answers before you start. You can move toward your goal, correct missteps before they become catastrophes, and build momentum toward rapid improvement.

When a Risk Fails

One test of a Side by Side leader is handling missteps. Failure to achieve a single goal does not make a failure of a person, team, or organization. What baseball player led the league in strikeouts? The same one who set the record for knocking it over the fence: Babe Ruth. Who missed the most game-winning baskets at the buzzer? Michael Jordan, the same superstar who *sank* the most game-winning baskets. Winners are the ones who try the most, risk the most, and learn the most from failure.

The risk in trying out new ideas is that sometimes it doesn't lead to success. However, it always leads to new knowledge — as Thomas Edison was fond of pointing out to his critics. Asked how he felt about a long series of failed experiments in pursuit of an important discovery, he replied, "I have not failed. I've just found 10,000 ways that won't work."

> The risk in trying out new ideas is that sometimes it doesn't lead to success. However, it always leads to new knowledge.

In businesses and other organizations, losing a calculated risk is not failure if the leader and the team gain new knowledge that can be used to achieve success the next time around. Frank Campbell, vice president of operations at Raytheon Montek in Salt Lake City, encouraged factory worker teams trained in structured team skills to take calculated risks. The teams consistently achieved 20 to 30 percent performance improvements, and everyone was content.

Eventually, one of the calculated risks resulted in a $20,000 loss. Uh-oh, people thought, Frank's gonna kill someone. But Frank stayed calm. He asked, quietly, "What did we learn from this?" There was a collective sigh of relief. The mistake had been turned into a knowledge asset.

Side by Side Tips

Learn and grow from all risks you take — especially the ones that fail. And remember to do the following:

- Filter creative ideas through the sieve of knowledge and experience.

- Use knowledge and experience to pick the best new ideas to further develop and put into action.

- Don't be afraid of risk; taking calculated risks creates new learning, which is the fountain of wealth.

- To evaluate a risky innovation, conduct a pilot test.

- Keep a positive, inquisitive attitude; failing is not failure if you learn from it.

Chapter 11

Principle 7:

Transferred Authority

Transferring Decision-Making Power Jump-Starts Action on New Ideas

A manufacturer of computer chips wanted to give more authority to make decisions to its mostly high school–educated machine operators. The managers asked an outside consultant to meet the workers with no supervisors present. The consultant asked, "What decisions would you like to make that your managers now make?" The workers listed about thirty. With the team's permission, the consultant shared the list with the team's managers.

The managers were shocked. "But they already have the power to make those decisions!" they said. "They always come in and check with one of us, or ask us to make the decision, but the power's theirs if they want to use it."

Why weren't the operators using the power the managers thought they had already given them? The consultant checked around and asked more questions. He discovered that things weren't as rosy as the managers claimed. Any employee who made a mistake was likely to be criticized, threatened, or even fired. The consultant also discovered that the machine operators knew about a problem that was costing the company $1 million a week, but they were afraid to tell their managers.

The essential ingredient that was missing was trust. Equipment operators were treated like children; their self-confidence was totally beaten down. On paper, they were empowered; but they didn't feel empowered, so they didn't act empowered.

The managers argued that the employees had to be treated like children because they behaved irresponsibly. This is a good example of a reciprocal leadership pattern. When leaders view and treat employees as children, employees' behavior adapts to fit the role, thus fulfilling leaders' expectations and reinforcing their behavior.

When leaders view and treat employees as children, employees' behavior adapts to fit the role.

The Side by Side Leadership model requires leaders to ask for the best thinking and ideas of their contributors on important issues that affect them. But because our culture has for centuries taken an authoritarian approach to leadership, contributors often don't know how to respond when a leader asks for their ideas.

When I was studying in Germany, some of my fellow exchange students and I got to meet Konrad Adenauer, the revered leader of post–World War II West Germany. The first thing he did was ask us our impressions of Germany. We were tongue-tied; this great man was interviewing us! He seemed genuinely interested in our opinions. When we spoke, his facial expressions and body language told us he was listening to, and thinking about, what we said. We felt important, significant, safe. We began to accept our empowerment.

Be Open, Supportive, and Patient

As a leader getting to know a new group of employees, keep in mind that most people are initially reluctant to be open and honest with their supervisors. The first time you ask for an employee's input, the ideas you get may be unusable, like rusty water from a long-unused faucet. The employee may criticize her own ideas, perhaps even throw out a bad idea or two on purpose, to test your openness and sincerity. But if you persist and demonstrate a sincere desire to hear and consider them, good ideas will begin to flow in a clear and refreshing stream. Be supportive; open your own ideas up for debate and discussion; show self-confidence, and encourage the contributor to be self-confident.

When the contributor appears to lack confidence, listen patiently but brush off any self-criticism. Studies have shown that discouraging negative self-talk can enhance the number and quality of ideas generated.[1] Criticism by others demonstrably hinders innovative thinking as well. In one study, bringing in outside observers to evaluate an innovative team function reduced the team's creativity, even when criticism was only a possibility.[2]

Contributors and leaders can influence each other's self-confidence. A leader promotes contributors' self-confidence by asking for, listening to, and supporting innovative thinking. One effective tool for the leader is the recognition event, in which employees are given the limelight and publicly applauded for their contributions. Another is for the leader to do an excellent job of performing tasks that contributors ask them to do. Contributors thus recognized are more likely to enhance leaders' self-confidence by listening to them and supporting their innovative thinking.

Share Authority Gradually

Sharing authority, though often awkward at first for both leaders and contributors, can be learned in small steps, the same way marksmen learn to hit a distant bullseye by starting close and gradually increasing their distance from the target. To build a contributor's confidence, start by assigning small but challenging tasks.[3] The experience of mastering stressful or challenging situations does more than simply build optimism — it creates what psychologists call self-efficacy, or a resourceful state.[4] A confident mind-set can be a launching pad for breakthrough.

Even thinking about past successes, remembering them in sensory detail, can boost self-confidence. A leader can instill confidence in subordinates by having them describe what they felt, thought, and did to overcome a challenge or achieve a goal. The recognition and the recalled experience reinforce each other and give the person the self-assurance to tackle even greater challenges.

Empower to Speed Implementation

Thinking up creative ideas is exciting, but employees and leaders alike are often frustrated by the time required to get an idea into action. Sometimes it takes so long that the

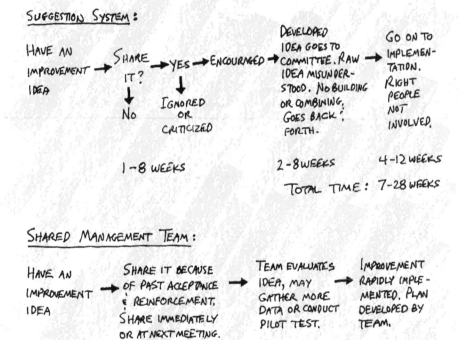

SUGGESTION SYSTEM:

HAVE AN IMPROVEMENT IDEA → SHARE IT? → YES → ENCOURAGED → DEVELOPED IDEA GOES TO COMMITTEE. RAW IDEA MISUNDER-STOOD. NO BUILDING OR COMBINING. GOES BACK ¢ FORTH. → GO ON TO IMPLEMEN-TATION. RIGHT PEOPLE NOT INVOLVED.

No → IGNORED OR CRITICIZED

1–8 WEEKS   2–8 WEEKS   4–12 WEEKS

TOTAL TIME: 7–28 WEEKS

SHARED MANAGEMENT TEAM:

HAVE AN IMPROVEMENT IDEA → SHARE IT BECAUSE OF PAST ACCEPTANCE ¢ REINFORCEMENT. SHARE IMMEDIATELY OR AT NEXT MEETING. → TEAM EVALUATES IDEA, MAY GATHER MORE DATA OR CONDUCT PILOT TEST. → IMPROVEMENT RAPIDLY IMPLE-MENTED. PLAN DEVELOPED BY TEAM.

1 HOUR – 1 WEEK   1 HOUR – 4 WEEKS   1 HOUR – 1 WEEK

TOTAL TIME: 3 HOURS – 6 WEEKS

idea is no longer useful or practical. This is often the case with the old-fashioned suggestion system, in which seven to twenty-four weeks typically elapse before implementation because of top-down management bottlenecks. The Side by Side system of shared-management work teams, by contrast, facilitates structured, creative discussions and decisions at all levels, which can lead to implementation within six weeks — or, in some cases, within hours!

Sharing leaders' goal-setting and decision-making responsibilities with employees not only speeds up the implementation of creative ideas, it leads to greater creativity in daily job tasks.[5] Employees take the responsibility for improving their own work processes; they think up better ways to do things, and they take the initiative to implement the improvements. This is the kind of improvement executives at the top of an organization never hear about — performance gets better, and nobody knows why. But the wise executive, the Side by Side leader who is in constant touch with contributors, knows why.

> Research and experience teach us that an organization should give all its members as much authority as possible.

What the research and experience teach us, as I showed in my earlier book *Breakthrough Teamwork*, is that an organization should give all its members as much authority as possible. Training contributors in team leadership skills, creative thinking, and specialized knowledge pays off almost immediately in higher performance.

It is wrong, however, to transfer authority without training. Managers who do so make the mistake of viewing empowerment as an employee light switch: flip, you're empowered. Unfortunately, it doesn't work that way. Giving employees more power without instilling in them the organization's visionary goals or giving them training in team skills and creative thinking simply induces chaos and confusion. The failure of unstructured empowerment has caused more than one top-down manager to justify micromanaging employees: "See, I told you they're like children."

Step by Step

Transitioning to structured empowerment is a gradual process of training and practicing. People earn more power by achieving outstanding results with each new increment of power they've been trained to use. The training starts with easy-to-learn ideas and skills. These can be taught in a few hours, like picking low-hanging fruit off a tree, and employees can be quickly empowered to use them to full advantage.

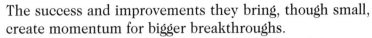

The success and improvements they bring, though small, create momentum for bigger breakthroughs.

Getting the hard-to-reach fruit at the top of the tree, however, takes more help and effort. More sophisticated creative thinking, problem solving, and idea implementation require more training and more power sharing. Greater challenges call for knowledge leadership from within and outside the organization. Cross-functional teams of leaders, organization members, customers, vendors, and even regulators facilitate the process. Harvesting the highest, sweetest fruit involves training, empowerment, cooperation, knowledge, and small successes that lead to ever larger successes.

Side by Side Tips

In sharing power, the following principles are key:

- To stimulate continuous innovation, support the flow of ideas and promote self-confidence.

- Build the trust of both leaders and contributors by gradually sharing more and more management authority.

- Provide structured team-skills training to enable team members to use their new authority effectively.

Part

III

Five Spheres of Influence and the Twenty Skills

The five spheres of influence in Side by Side Leadership express themselves through twenty identifiable and teachable skills. In the next five chapters, these skills are discussed and explained in terms of the most reliable research that has been conducted and the most practical aspects of applying them to your professional situation. Examples of how top leaders in different types of organizations have developed and applied them will help you see their function and significance in achieving visionary goals.

PERSONAL **LEADERSHIP**	Skill 1: Achieving Personal Visionary Goals Skill 2: Practicing Honesty and Fairness Skill 3: Maintaining Objectivity
KNOWLEDGE **LEADERSHIP**	Skill 4: Acquiring Knowledge Skill 5: Sharing Knowledge Skill 6: Transforming Knowledge
INTERPERSONAL **LEADERSHIP**	Skill 7: Two-Way Listening Skill 8: Mutual Contributing Skill 9: Connecting Visionary Goals Skill 10: Diverse Networking
TEAM **LEADERSHIP**	Skill 11: Managing the Interface Skill 12: Setting Team Goals Skill 13: Using Structured Team Skills Skill 14: Coordinating Team Roles Skill 15: Increasing Team Capacity
ORGANIZATIONAL **LEADERSHIP**	Skill 16: Identifying Opportunities and Threats Skill 17: Living Organizational Values Skill 18: Setting Organizational Visionary Goals Skill 19: Creating New Strategies Skill 20: Creating a Flexible Organization

Chapter 12

Sphere 1:

Personal Leadership

Leading by Maintaining Personal Integrity and Setting a Strong Example for Contributors

Mohandas Gandhi had no organization. He held no political office. He had few possessions. He renounced the use of violence. His most frightening weapon was starving himself. Yet Mohandas Gandhi led millions of people in India — Great Britain's largest colony, the Jewel in the Crown — to an almost bloodless independence. His nonviolent civil disobedience became a model for leaders seeking political, racial, and religious freedom around the world.

What was it about Gandhi that made him such a compelling and magnetic leader? He was a remarkable person in many ways, but certainly the most striking facet of his leadership was his personal influence on the people who knew him and the millions who followed him. This intense personal leadership influence was grounded in his total, uncompromising commitment to his values — honesty and love.

Gandhi is an excellent example for the personal sphere of Side by Side Leadership. Leaders need firm, unwavering personal values and goals. Whatever your other leadership attributes, personal leadership is at the center. It is with you every moment of the day. It is the rock upon which all your other leadership capabilities rest, the guiding force that keeps your leadership goals and practices in line with your values.

Side by Side Leadership works best when both leaders and contributors have well-developed personal values and goals and exert strong personal leadership influence. Managers with poorly defined personal values and goals usually display weak personal leadership; they're the ones who take opinion polls before saying what they think. They are hard to pin down, easily influenced by others, and instill little confidence in their employees and colleagues. They may try or pretend to be effective in all the other spheres of Side by Side Leadership, but their results will be limited and temporary. The leader with weak personal leadership skills cannot be truly Side by Side; strong contributors will overpower him.

In this chapter we will discuss three skills you can use to develop your personal leadership ability:

Skill 1: Achieving personal visionary goals

Skill 2: Practicing honesty and fairness

Skill 3: Maintaining objectivity

Skill 1: Achieving Personal Visionary Goals

Psychiatrist Victor Frankl, a survivor of the World War II Nazi death camps, both studied and exemplified the importance of having a goal to which you can daily commit yourself. As a medical doctor and scientist, Frankl rose above his role as an inmate and became a perceptive observer, recorder, and analyzer of his fellow sufferers.

In his book *Man's Search for Meaning*, Frankl described the horrors and deprivations of life in the camps — harsh winters, little clothing, inadequate shelter, meager rations. He posed the question: What was the difference between those who survived and those who died? The answer was his major discovery. Those who survived had a vision or major goal they were committed to achieving. People with this sense of daily purpose seemed to have a stronger immune system and were less likely to fall victim to the camp's many diseases. Frankl credits his own survival to a fierce devotion to his own goal: to write a book on his new theory of mental and emotional health.

Among the twentieth century's most creative writers, artists, scientists, and businesspeople that he studied, University of Chicago psychology professor Mihaly Csikszentmihalyi (chapter 8) found great differences in knowledge, experience, and leadership style, but one attribute in common: they loved their work. "It is not the hope of achieving fame or of making money that drives them; rather, it is the opportunity to do the work they enjoy doing."[1] Because they love their work, successful people spend a lot of time doing it.

In earlier research on happiness and motivation, Csikszentmihalyi discovered a phenomenon he called "flow," which he defined as "the state in which people are so involved in an activity nothing else seems to matter; the experience itself is so enjoyable that people will do it even at great cost, for the sheer sake of doing it."[2]

Prioritize Your Goals

As a leadership consultant, I have met many talented people who had ambitious, challenging, yet achievable goals, but who found success elusive. What stopped them? It became apparent that they were trying to excel in too many endeavors at once instead

> THREE KEY FACTORS THAT HELP YOU ACHIEVE FLOW:
>
> • CLEAR, SPECIFIC GOALS
> • THE ABILITY TO EASILY MEASURE PROGRESS TOWARD YOUR GOALS
> • CONTROL OVER THE DEGREE OF CHALLENGE IN YOUR GOALS
>
> THE THREE FACTORS THAT PROMOTE WORK HAPPINESS OR "FLOW" ALSO IMPROVE WORK PERFORMANCE. YOU CAN MAKE YOUR WORK ENGAGING AND SATISFYING BY SETTING STRETCH GOALS THAT ARE JUST BARELY ACHIEVABLE.

of focusing on just one or a few goals and sticking with them until they were achieved.

In an interesting study of leadership in Europe, researchers at IBM found that organizations that focused on only a few goals at a time experienced greater success than those focusing on ten or more goals. I believe the same principle applies to individuals: high achievers typically pursue only a few goals at a time — but with laserlike focus.

Through his Covey Leadership Center, Stephen Covey *(Seven Habits of Highly Effective People)* studied organizations worldwide that won the highly coveted Deming Prize for quality in products and services and found that their executives spent over half their days focused on strategic activities in pursuit of major organizational goals. The average executive, by contrast, spent only 15 percent of the day in strategic pursuits.[3] It appears to me that the successful executives had the time to be strategic because they delegated much of their authority for work they deemed less important.

Achieving success is not a complicated thing. Just dedicate fifty hours a week to your highest-priority goals, and you'll get there.

Be Specific

At least twenty solid research studies have proved that wording goals very specifically yields 20 percent greater success than setting vague or overly broad goals. Locke and other industrial psychologists found that performance was enhanced when the target was a specific quantity, as opposed to "do your best." Thomas Edison wanted to be the greatest inventor of his time. He set a specific goal: patent a new invention every month. He beat that target; over the course of his life he obtained 1,093 patents, including those for the electric light bulb and the phonograph.

When you formulate your few personal goals, apply the principles for developing visionary goals presented in chapter 7. Envision in full what you want to achieve; set the bar high; write it down. To achieve the goal, be creative and work side by side with people who share your goals. Regularly measure your progress toward the goal, using graphs, tables, whatever works. You'll find that developing and working toward visionary goals can be fun, especially when you can see that you're moving steadily closer to achieving them, and your enthusiasm will draw contributors to your cause like a magnet.

Skill 2: Practicing Honesty and Fairness

Tell people the truth, because they know the truth anyway.

— Jack Welch, CEO, General Electric[4]

How would you like it if, no matter how large your organization grew, your customers would travel for nine hours to buy products and services from you? Ray Shepard's customers do just that. They drive in from other states to buy a car from his Ford dealership in Ft. Scott, Kansas.

Ray Shepard began acquiring his reputation for honesty and fairness back in the '50s. Before he took customers out to see his new and used cars, he would ask them what they were looking for, then match their wishes with the cars he had on hand. He kept prices as low as possible to give the customer a good deal yet still allow himself a small profit. People trusted his service department, too. No one worried about spending money on unnecessary repairs.

Nearby dealerships couldn't compete, and Ray gradually absorbed several General Motors, Chrysler, and Toyota outlets. Now customers make great pilgrimages to buy new and used cars from Ray Shepard's Team Auto. They leave happy and relaxed, because they know they got a fair deal from an honest man.

> **HOW TO BEHAVE FAIRLY IN ANY INTERACTION:**
>
> - TALK OVER YOUR CONCERNS WITH OTHERS AS EQUALS.
> - LISTEN TO THE VALUES & DESIRES OF OTHERS.
> - CALMLY STATE WHAT YOU THINK IS FAIR FOR YOURSELF.
> - KEEP LISTENING & ADDING BACKGROUND INFORMATION TO THE ISSUE.

Many leaders think that being fair to others means sacrificing your own goals, but top leaders know that it's easier to be fair with others when you're being treated fairly. If you're achieving your visionary goals day by day, you're less likely to feel you're being taken advantage of, and more likely to react fairly and generously toward others and help them achieve their goals. In the ideal outcome, as in Ray Shepard's business dealings, everyone comes out ahead. Fairness is a mutual benefit of a healthy Side by Side relationship.

Honesty Breeds Trust

Honesty is being friends with reality. The honest leader recognizes what exists, good or bad, as a resource for achieving goals. Practicing dishonesty is like trying to see life through glasses smudged with dirt and grease — you can't see the golden opportunities and resourceful people right in front of you. Leaders who treat others unfairly are always looking over their shoulder, worried they're going to get caught. This distracts them from looking forward and seeing the future.

Honesty is being friends with reality. The honest leader recognizes what exists, good or bad, as a resource for achieving goals.

Many ethical standards vary from person to person — for example, those specific to one's religious beliefs. But two leadership virtues are universal: honesty and fairness. Different people may have different definitions of these two words, but Don Stacy, president of Amoco Canada, stated his expectations in clear terms. He told his managers, "Don't lie, cheat, or steal." His simple admonition replaced hundreds of pages of policy and procedure manuals.

Thomas Stanley, author of the 1996 bestseller *The Millionaire Next Door,* published a recent study in which self-made millionaires, asked to rate thirty success factors for achieving wealth, rated "being honest with all people" number one. They knew that persuading people to invest large sums of money required, above all, earning their trust.

The same is true of any large endeavor, including governments. National leaders with high ethical standards achieve greater prosperity for their citizens than dishonest leaders.[5, 6] Investors will risk money and time in economies whose leaders, vendors, and customers they feel they can trust. Most of the economic development in the former Soviet Union has occurred in countries that enforce laws and ethical standards.

Some managers still have trouble believing honesty is good business; some choose to be dishonest with customers or employees, believing it gives them a business advantage. However, asked if they want their own employees to be dishonest with them or the organization, they say "No!" Nobody wants to work with dishonest people, but people who do either withhold their best efforts or, in the worst cases, follow the example set for them by their bosses. If the leader's behavior is ethical, contributors tend to be ethical, too.[7]

Life and business today move too fast to waste months drawing up ironclad contracts; people have to act quickly, and in order for that to happen, leaders and contributors have to trust each other. The "virtual corporation" exists largely on trust; the best people choose up sides and work with others they can trust. The leaders of the best companies pick trustworthy customers and suppliers to quickly develop new and improved products and services. Without information they can trust, leaders cannot take the calculated risks that create wealth.

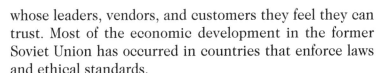

The best people choose up sides and work with others they can trust.

Gandhi's honesty was one of his strongest leadership tools. It was not a calculated skill but a natural outgrowth of his integrity. One day a mother, concerned that her teenage son was eating too much sugar, brought the boy to visit Gandhi. The great man listened to her complaint, then told the mother to bring him back in one month. When she did so, Gandhi looked the son in the eye, shook his finger in the boy's face, and said, "Don't eat so much sugar!" The mother, puzzled, asked Gandhi why he had waited a month to speak to her son. Gandhi replied, "A month ago, I ate too much sugar."

Moral leaders like Gandhi, Martin Luther King Jr., Jesus, Moses, Mohammed, Buddha, and Confucius are the most enduring for humankind because their leadership changed the interaction field of all of society, where organizations, families, and individuals must survive and thrive. Whether you are the next Gandhi or the next Ray Shepard, you can achieve more than you ever dreamed by working at always being honest and fair.

Skill 3: Maintaining Objectivity

If you can keep your head when all about you are losing theirs . . . Yours is the Earth and everything that's in it. . . .

— Rudyard Kipling, "If"[8]

Maintaining emotional balance means not letting emotions overwhelm objective thinking. Sometimes the leader is like the captain of a ship in stormy emotional seas. Objectivity is the compass that, whatever the weather or sea conditions, tells the captain where to steer to reach the organization's visionary goals.

When problems arise, it is critically important that the leader preserve objective thinking. Leaders who are emotionally balanced can, when in crisis, remain objective and think lucidly, even creatively. Leaders who become anxious or angry, however, tend to lose their problem-solving skills, forget crucial information, and think inside the box. They lash out at others, blind to the damage they are doing. Worse, they sometimes begin to behave top-down, retreating into the office, dictating orders, taking back power they previously delegated. This cuts them off from the very problem-solving resources that might save them — the minds of contributors.

The effects of uncontrolled emotion can be disastrous for both leaders and contributors. According to findings of Personnel Decisions, Inc. and the Center for Creative Leadership, two of the nation's top leadership assessment organizations, highly capable technical and knowledge leaders sometimes fail in their overall leadership effectiveness because they are perceived by contributors and other managers as being too emotional.[9] Other research shows that unmanaged emotional stress gets in the way of creativity.[10]

In extreme situations, uncontrolled emotions can even be hazardous to your health. Frequent anger is a probable risk factor for heart attacks. Anger reduces heart efficiency 5 to 7 percent, with 7 percent being clinically dangerous. Reduced heart efficiency in turn affects blood flow to the brain, which hurts creativity and high-order thinking. In heart attack patients, training to reduce the intensity and frequency of anger has been shown to lower by 44 percent the incidence of a second heart attack.[11] Learning to manage your anger not only makes you a better leader, it can extend your life.

Bowen Natural Systems Theory (chapter 2) states that a person in an emotional or anxious situation can reduce his stress and potential health problems by becoming a neutral researcher and asking questions of himself. Another, less emphasized, reason that Victor Frankl survived the death camps may have been that he became an unemotional observer of his own behavior and situation. Recent brain research summarized by Dr. John Allman found that stress chemicals in the brain decrease when a person becomes an objective problem solver.[12]

Anger reduces heart efficiency 5 to 7 percent, with 7 percent being clinically dangerous.

Poise under Pressure

Simply presenting a calm demeanor in times of crisis makes leaders more effective.[13] You know this intuitively. Remember the time you stepped on a broken bottle and cut your foot wide open? One of your friends panicked and ran off, but the other stayed calm, wrapped your foot in a towel, and called your mom to come get you. His presence reassured you and kept you from being frightened.

Psychologist Irving Janus has shown that poor decision makers are reluctant to face threats head-on. Emotional balance helps leaders face threats as rational facts rather than irrational stresses. Staying calm helps keep your brain supplied with oxygen and lets you view the situation as it really is and take appropriate action. It allows you to see the big picture, which includes the different interaction

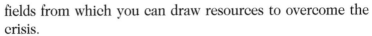

fields from which you can draw resources to overcome the crisis.

In the 1980s, Intel Corporation, the premier producer of computer chips, was in the middle of a slow-motion business disaster. The company was losing its shirt to Japanese competitors in the computer memory business. Because it had been a pioneering designer and producer of memory, this failure was especially bitter for Intel and its leaders, which included Andy Grove and CEO Gordon Moore.

One day Grove asked Moore, "If the board fired us and brought in new people, what would the new CEO do?" Moore replied that the new leader would get Intel out of the computer memory business.

Grove then calmly suggested that he and Moore walk out the door of their executive office suite, then walk back in and take that action themselves.[14]

Grove and Moore did indeed pull Intel out of its money-losing memory chip business. There followed many months of agonizing decisions and false starts, but eventually Intel threw all its resources into microprocessors, and a string of triumphs with its 286, 386, 486, Pentium, and Pentium II modules helped Intel grow 40 percent a year for a solid decade. Andy Grove's coolly objective question had resolved an organizational crisis and set Intel on track to become one of America's most successful businesses. For his calm and objective reactions in time of crisis, as well as his subsequent top-notch leadership as Intel's CEO, *Time* magazine named Grove its 1997 Person of the Year.

Personal Stress Management

To lead calmly and objectively when problems arise at work, you need to be able to manage stress in your personal life. Maintaining emotional balance means balancing the four components of emotion: physical, social, mental, and spiritual.

Physical balance comes from exercise and recreation. Whether you prefer walking, jogging, swimming, or skipping rope, the value of physical exercise for managing stress is

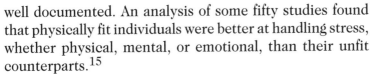

well documented. An analysis of some fifty studies found that physically fit individuals were better at handling stress, whether physical, mental, or emotional, than their unfit counterparts.[15]

Social balance is about how you apportion your time between being alone and being with other people. Different personalities define this balance in different ways. An extrovert may need lots of time with family, co-workers, and friends; introverts need time alone to reenergize themselves. A leader whose job involves a great deal of people contact may need more alone time on weekends.

Everyone needs a network of relationships, not only to help solve problems and accomplish goals but to reduce stress. Leaders, in particular, need both professional and personal friends to buffer the stress and emotional pressures of leadership.[16]

Mental balance involves the mix of intellectual challenge and contemplative time in your life. Most leaders need plenty of mental stimulation during the week; unchallenged by constructive activity, their minds can turn inward and become self-destructive. College-educated housewives or househusbands who stay home to raise young children often find themselves under great stress from lack of intellectual stimulation. Their thinking turns self-critically inward.

If you notice your thinking becoming overly analytical and negative about yourself or others, you may need to immerse your mind in some mentally challenging activity. Reading books, attending classes, listening to music, going to plays strictly for pleasure — these things not only give the mind something fresh and new to contemplate, they keep the leader attuned to the cultural lives of associates, customers, contributors, and friends.

Spiritual balance is not necessarily about religion but about taking time during the week to relax, thinking about the good things in your life, and feeling grateful just to be alive. Spiritual balance comes from tuning your eyes to the sunset, your ears to birdsong, your nose to the roses outside your window. Harvard Professor Herbert Benson, M.D. conducted thirty years of research on the health benefits of spiritual balance. He found that twenty minutes a day spent in meditation, prayer, or quiet thinking reduced blood pressure, heart rate, breathing rate, and muscle tension, and brought improvements in fifteen different medical problem areas. In his latest book, *Timeless Healing,* Benson states: "Our bodies are wired to benefit from exercising not only our muscles but our rich inner, human core — our beliefs, values, thoughts, and feelings."[17]

Maintaining physical, social, mental, and spiritual balance helps leaders stay centered. It lets them manage the strong emotions and stresses inherent in leading others.

Daily Discipline

Many leaders achieve success, but those who maintain it without succumbing to its temptations typically practice some daily discipline. Benjamin Franklin, who was both financially and socially influential, kept a list of values and habits for self-improvement and spent time each day reviewing how well he had adhered to them. Gandhi prayed and meditated for an hour every morning, asking himself how faithfully he had observed his two main values, love and honesty, the previous day.

Maintaining the discipline of daily physical exercise is a habit practiced by many successful leaders. Dr. Carl Rogers, a founder of Counseling Psychology, swam every day. Harry Truman established an unvarying habit of taking a brisk walk in the morning, long before he became president. He kept it up during and after his presidency, well into his seventies, often outpacing the young reporters who followed and asked questions.

These leaders knew that, whatever the day's triumphs and tribulations, they were at least maintaining a daily discipline of one of their values. Their routines gave them a sense of control, buffering the physical and emotional stresses of leading others.[18]

Chapter 13

Sphere 2:

Knowledge Leadership

Leading by Seeking, Developing, Extending, Sharing, and Harnessing Knowledge

Knowledge can be thought of as information filtered through experience that can be applied. It is more than just facts; as Stan Davis and Jim Botkin wrote in their book *The Monster under the Bed,* "Knowledge is information put to productive use."[1] And who is it that guides it into productive use? The knowledge leader.

Knowledge leadership is an important part of Side by Side Leadership. It is the ability to use knowledge to get work done and achieve visionary goals that distinguishes this facet of leadership. It is an essential part of the formula for achieving outstanding team and organizational results.

An organization can apply all its other leadership resources — organizational, team, interpersonal, and personal — toward a goal and still fail to achieve it. What's missing? Quite likely, knowledge leadership. And it's not just high-tech companies that need it; specialized knowledge and experience is needed in most endeavors, including human services.

In an evaluation of 100 innovative community programs for juvenile delinquents and youth at risk, fewer than five were found to be successful. No matter how charismatic, creative, and inspirational the leaders were, most of the new programs failed. They failed to do their homework; they repeated mistakes that had been made in the past. Studies had already shown that although teaching youths accountability and practical interpersonal and living skills reduced the number of offenses, recreation and counseling by themselves proved ineffective.[2] Having and using this knowledge would have saved these communities a lot of money and wasted effort.

A knowledge leader is sometimes pictured as a lone genius working feverishly in a dark laboratory. University of Michigan professors Donald Pelz and Frank Andrews shot down this "mad scientist" myth. Their research showed that the most productive scientists and engineers were those who interacted the most with colleagues inside and outside the organization, using their contacts to confirm their ideas and acquire new knowledge.[3] This has been done traditionally by presenting findings at conferences and in journals. In today's world, however, next month or next year is too late. Real-time, personal contact with knowledge originators has become the method of choice, whether in person, by phone, or via the Internet.

In my experience, the best knowledge leaders are those who master and apply these three skills:

Skill 4: Acquiring knowledge

Skill 5: Sharing knowledge

Skill 6: Transforming knowledge

Skill 4: Acquiring Knowledge

Side by Side knowledge leaders are skilled at working with others to acquire and apply knowledge toward team and organization goals. In particular, there are three kinds of knowledge that are of value to the organization: work savvy, organizational savvy, and professional or technical savvy.

Research has shown that success on the job is directly related to a person's knowledge of how to get things done. Yale University psychologist Robert Sternberg, who called this ability "tacit knowledge" or "practical intelligence," found that managerial performance among bank managers and business managers was 150 percent more closely related to their work savvy and organizational savvy than to their general intelligence or "IQ."

Work savvy is, in general, knowing how to complete a work task. Individuals with work savvy

- know the steps necessary to complete the work task,

- perform each step ably and well,

- recognize that completing each step as quickly and efficiently as possible is important to overall productivity, and

- understand that quality is important no matter how fast one works.

Knowledge leaders typically stay busy doing their work, out of sight of others, often silent during meetings, but their co-workers know who they are and search them out when they get stuck. They develop efficient, effective work processes that enhance quality and productivity — the "best practices" and "future practices" that other companies strive to emulate.

New employees with work savvy tend to hit the ground running. Microsoft found that college students who had worked their way through school while maintaining high grade point averages had a winning combination of work savvy and technical savvy.

Organizational savvy is the ability to perform complex tasks or projects using resources inside or outside the organization. Individuals with high organizational savvy get results by working across organizational boundaries and outside their own work groups, teaming up with people and resources both inside and outside the organization to achieve their goals. They know

- how to involve other people in the work,

- how to pick up where others left off,

- how to pass the work along, and
- how work is connected to the organization's business model for success.

In the 1980s, Boeing Aircraft hired young professionals as prospective managers and knowledge leaders. The company trained them in "the Boeing Way," starting with an overview of how to use Boeing's people, departments, and resources to get work done. Dell Computer used a different approach in the 1990s; it trained current employees in the Dell business model. Dell employees learned how their work connected with Dell's processes for satisfying customers and making money. Both Boeing and Dell increased their employees' organizational savvy to achieve better results faster.

Professional and technical savvy is knowledge acquired in college or technical training or by reading books. Technical knowledge is used in all areas of work, from accounting to zinc plating.

Proven Knowledge

There are times when it is especially important for a leader to do her homework and seek to increase her knowledge

- when going to work for a new company,
- when getting a new job assignment or a promotion, or
- when major changes have occurred in her field of knowledge or in the business climate.

It's important to acquire and use knowledge selectively. Even when trying to keep up with rapid changes in the business environment has you stressed out, don't let desperation drive you to accept information uncritically. Knowledge is highly variable in quality. Don't be swayed by fads and trends that have not been shown to make a real difference. Look for high-quality, proven knowledge that has measurably improved performance when applied.

Where should you look? You're more likely to uncover useful knowledge if you focus your search in certain areas:

Industry-leading organizations. Visit the top companies; observe their processes; see how their people apply their knowledge and skills. (You can contact these leading organizations through your local chamber of commerce or the industry trade association.) Which parts of the process are most responsible for the company's outstanding results? This kind of evaluation is known as benchmarking. Many American executives laughed when visiting Japanese business leaders benchmarked American industries in the '60s and '70s, carrying cameras and snapping pictures as fast as they could wind the film. They finally stopped laughing in the '80s when the companies the Japanese led surpassed their U.S. counterparts. (Think Sony and Toyota.)

Experts. Most of the knowledge creators in any field are only three phone calls or e-mails away. First, ask anyone in the new field you are interested in to name someone he knows who is a top expert. Then call the expert and ask who has had the best success using the knowledge. This gets you your third contact — an expert who knows how to apply the knowledge.

Hard-data research. Technical journals and proceedings in university libraries, especially up-to-the-minute online versions, can put you at the cutting edge of knowledge. Sometimes professors who conduct or keep track of research projects can be of help. Check university web sites for the names of experts in your area of specialized knowledge.

When I was helping Motorola develop a training course in goal setting, I discovered "Mr. Goal Setting" himself — Professor Edwin Locke of the University of Maryland, who had conducted more hard research on corporate goal setting than anyone. I called him, and he consulted with me on his yet-to-be-published findings, which I used to create a successful goal-setting course.

Yourself. Create the knowledge on your own by comparing, combining, and analyzing the results of other people's research studies and by performing your own experiments. You will then become a knowledge leader, and others will share their knowledge in exchange for yours.

WHY SIDE BY SIDE LEADERS SHARE KNOWLEDGE	WHY TOP-DOWN MANAGERS HOARD KNOWLEDGE
THEY BELIEVE THAT SHARED KNOWLEDGE MAKES IT EASIER FOR ALL TO DO THEIR JOBS BETTER.	THEY BELIEVE THAT KNOWLEDGE IS POWER AND MUST BE CONTROLLED TIGHTLY TO MAINTAIN THEIR AUTHORITY.
THEY EXPAND THEIR KNOWLEDGE BY EXCHANGING INFORMATION WITH CONTRIBUTORS.	THEY COMMUNICATE KNOWLEDGE ONE WAY ONLY, IN MONOLOGUES AND LECTURES. THEY ASSUME LISTENERS KNOW NOTHING ABOUT THE TOPIC AND THERE IS NO REASON TO HAVE THE LISTENERS PARTICIPATE BEYOND ALLOWING THEM TO ASK A FEW QUESTIONS.

Whatever method you use to acquire proven knowledge, always keep in mind your personal, team, and organizational goals and let them steer your learning. Then apply the knowledge with the goals firmly fixed in your mind.

Skill 5: Sharing Knowledge

As a Side by Side leader, your goal will never be to control access to your specialized knowledge, but to share it with colleagues and contributors in pursuit of common goals. In this respect, Side by Side knowledge leaders differ markedly from top-down leaders.

The best knowledge leaders share what they know. In return, they ask for and receive the benefit of the knowledge, experience, and insights of others.

Everyone's Need to Know

Dave Williams, former executive leader of Moog's aircraft parts division in Salt Lake City, maintained that one role of organizational leaders is to share knowledge about the business with all employees. Dave thought that the more contributors knew about how each part of the business was performing, the better would be their suggestions and improvements for their own parts of the organization.

John Case documents the business benefits of sharing financial data in *Open-Book Management*.[4] Organizational performance and financial information should be communicated interactively rather than in authoritarian, one-way presentations. One leadership team put some fun into their quarterly progress report meetings by presenting them in a quiz-show format and inviting "contestants" from the audience to guess the results.

Leaders develop other knowledge leaders through training and education. In the 1980s, organizations that had the most and broadest employee training, like Ford (80 hours/year/employee), gained the most in quality. General Electric and Cisco Systems emphasized employee training and experienced dramatic growth in the 1990s.

Here are ways you can share your knowledge to help your organization achieve outstanding results:

Capsulize. Knowledge leaders sometimes find it hard to communicate their vast wealth of information to others, especially those with little background in their field. The best way around this roadblock is to organize the information in packets — small, self-contained capsules of knowledge that can be easily transferred and applied for immediate results. Knowledge that is addressed to performing specific tasks and achieving specific goals is the most readily applied.

Psychologist Robert Carkhuff discovered that knowledge packaged as short principles and skill steps is easiest for contributors to personalize and put to use. I've read a lot of books about time management, but what I remember best — and use daily — are two simple skills: budgeting time for my highest priorities, and writing down appointments in my pocket planner.

Coach. Side by Side coaching transfers knowledge to contributors who are given new work assignments or whose

> Knowledge that is addressed to performing specific tasks and achieving specific goals is the most readily applied.

work performance is lagging. A mutual coaching session to teach a skill should be structured — that is, it should have an agenda.

Leaders who take the time to share their expertise side by side with contributors in skill practice coaching sessions are, in effect, bequeathing their success to the future. The two-way nature of this process is vital; at each step, the leader asks the contributor for his thoughts, questions, and ideas. If a picture is worth a thousand words, then hands-on coaching, demonstration, practice, and two-way feedback on a work skill is worth ten thousand words.

To COACH A NEW SKILL:

- DISCUSS EACH SKILL STEP AND REASONS FOR USING IT.
- DEMONSTRATE THE STEPS.
- LET THE LEARNER PRACTICE.
- GIVE FEEDBACK SIDE BY SIDE.

Clarify. A key requirement in communicating expert knowledge is to use language and examples the learner can comprehend. Albert Einstein made relativity understandable to the average person with a clear and simple picture: two people throwing a ball back and forth on a moving train. To communicate their ideas, the great moral and religious teachers of civilization — Jesus, Mohammed, Moses, Buddha, Confucius, Lao Tzu — translated their life principles into simple but powerful words and stories about fishermen, farmers, and shepherds.

The same principle applies for communication between specialties. Multidisciplinary teams function better when each member communicates her specialized knowledge in language that team members from other disciplines can understand.

The Side by Side Advantage

Although training is widely recognized as the fastest route to record-setting results, many leaders and contributors are uncomfortable training others. They're afraid of saying something stupid or being ridiculed. Side by Side

Leadership makes training less stressful by implementing structured sessions in which all participants share the load. No one person is responsible for contributing all the information, knowledge, creativity, and best thinking; leaders and contributors share these things mutually.

The leader's most important function is to make sure learners practice the new skills and apply the new information to actual work, and that all the people on the team who must work toward a common goal are trained at the same time. In cross-functional teams, with members from different departments, this training is especially important.

Skill 6: Transforming Knowledge

The 1990s saw an explosion of knowledge-based services and products, provided and produced by knowledge workers. A new term arose for the valuable new commodity that was generated: intellectual capital. In Side by Side Leadership, "intellectual capital" is defined as knowledge shared

HOW TO TURN INTELLECTUAL CAPITAL INTO A SUCCESSFUL BUSINESS VENTURE:

- DEVELOP VISIONARY GOALS FOR THE NEW VENTURE.
- START SMALL TO ACHIEVE EARLY RESULTS RAPIDLY.
- CREATE PROVEN RESULTS THROUGH EXPERIMENTATION & EVALUATION.
- DOCUMENT & IMPROVE WORK PROCESSES THAT SUPPORT THE SUCCESS OF SERVICES OR PRODUCTS.
- BUILD SIDE BY SIDE TEAMS WITH CUSTOMERS & KNOWLEDGE LEADERS.
- DOCUMENT & PUBLICIZE THE SUCCESS OF THE IMPROVED SERVICES & PRODUCTS.

among two or more people that can be used to produce new products and services that achieve documented business results.

Here are some key elements for converting intellectual capital into successful business ventures:

Develop visionary goals. Workers in top-down, competitive cultures are possessive with knowledge, unwilling to share their tricks of the trade. Why should they? Wouldn't that just put them out of a job? On the other hand, I've seen old, stodgy, dying organizations reborn when their leaders and contributors committed themselves to achieving one or two shared visionary goals — goals that express the ideals they would like their company to achieve.

To achieve visionary goals takes more than business as usual; people *must* share knowledge. Visionary goals also stimulate new knowledge, because people gain recognition for inventing new ways to achieve them.

Start small. Product development research has shown time and time again that the company that's first out with a new product or service usually profits the most from it. But a company that has no shared vision and fears failure can easily waste twelve to eighteen months overanalyzing a possible new venture, and thereby lose a valuable opportunity.

How do successful companies overcome this "analysis paralysis"? Dorothy Leonard's book *Wellsprings of Knowledge* tells how.[5] They begin by experimenting on a small scale, through pilot programs. Workers, customers, vendors, and partners who will help grow the business should be encouraged to contribute some part of the knowledge that will be brought together to make the endeavor a success. The Side by Side knowledge leader is the one who makes the pieces come together.

Create proven results through experimentation and evaluation. Pilot experiments provide raw data about what works and what doesn't; evaluations create new, more refined knowledge that can be used to improve the quality and reduce the costs of a service or product, and perhaps to expand the business venture itself. The process is useful in any industry, from computer chips to potato chips — what is it, exactly, about the taste of those things that makes this brand more popular than that one?

Besides rapidly creating additional business knowledge, pilot tests are useful sales tools. They can be used to show prospective customers the superiority of the new service or product.

Document and improve the work processes that support the success of the services or products. When Ray Kroc bought the successful McDonald's fast-food business from its founders, one of his first actions was to document how the work was being done. These details, including all the steps required to turn out McDonald's delicious, hot, crispy french fries, are now preserved in the company's "playbook."

Knowledge leaders in any company need to work effectively with the specialists who compile and improve the company's playbook. The 1990s saw a huge movement toward reengineering organizations to improve their work processes. To do so effectively, people needed to share knowledge openly and evaluate processes critically. However, many process improvement teams failed to do this, or recommended only inconsequential changes, the equivalent of rearranging the deck chairs on the *Titanic.*

Build Side by Side teams with customers and knowledge leaders. To document and improve the playbook for new and growing businesses, teams need to turn on the flow of creative ideas from all team members. Cultivating openness and trust will continuously improve results by encouraging everyone to create and share knowledge.

To fully realize the gains from this new knowledge requires communicating with customers to learn and understand their needs. As Karl Sveiby wrote, "Success in the delicate business of transferring human competence . . . depends to a very large extent on how well knowledge vendors communicate with their customers."[6] Teamwork with customers promotes even faster improvement and expansion of new moneymaking businesses.

Document and publicize the success of the improved services and products. Two Minnesota doctors, brothers Will and Charlie Mayo, started a two-person practice in Rochester, Minnesota, that became one of the world's leading medical centers and now treats more than 400,000 patients a year. They did so by keeping abreast of medical discoveries, attending medical conferences and procedural demonstrations worldwide, and converting the knowledge into new business. They collected follow-up data on all their procedures. Each time they publicized their success rates, upwards of 90 percent, they attracted a whole new population of patients.

The Mayo brothers had their own formula for success:

- They learned innovative techniques and treatments from others to stimulate their own innovations.

- They documented their treatment of each patient, including any new techniques used and the immediate results.

- They followed up and evaluated the results of all treatments.

- They applied their findings and continuously improved their medical techniques.

- They recruited the best students and medical professionals they could find.

- They attracted worldwide attention through their success in treating difficult medical problems.

The Mayo brothers established good relationships with newspapers in their state and in large cities worldwide. They used easy-to-understand press releases to report their impressive success rates in treating serious illnesses. The publicity brought famous people to Rochester, further increasing the credibility and growth of the clinic. Time has proven the Mayo brothers two of the most successful knowledge leaders in history.

Chapter 14

Sphere 3:

Interpersonal Leadership

Leading by Listening Effectively, Contributing Unselfishly, Motivating Charismatically, and Networking Diversely

Leadership at its most basic level requires face-to-face time between two people. In the typical organization, managers spend 40 to 60 percent of their day interacting with other people; executives, 90 percent.[1, 2] These interactions are crucial. Even if all other spheres of leadership are working, leadership is destined to fail if the interpersonal connection cannot be made to function. Two top national leadership assessment organizations, the Center for Creative Leadership and Personnel Decisions, Inc., found that even managers and executives with high knowledge and technical expertise can fail when they are inept in their interpersonal interactions. It's a major derailer of careers.

Conversely, leaders who excel in interpersonal influence can compensate for shortcomings in other spheres. Research detailed in Daniel Goleman's book *Emotional Intelligence* shows the importance of interpersonal skills in achieving success in work and life.

Interpersonal leadership is a complex phenomenon; who knows why some people exert a magnetic attraction while others disappear behind their own shadow? No two interpersonal styles are alike, but it is possible to define four skills in particular that contribute to effective interpersonal leadership:

Skill 7: Two-Way Listening

Side by Side Leadership rests upon a foundation of listening to contributors (chapter 2). You can easily see the effects of good interpersonal listening skills in action. Watch when a contributor presents an idea; the Side by Side leader faces the contributor, looks at her, and concentrates on what she is saying. Then he restates what she said to see if he understands. The contributor listens attentively to the leader. When the conversation ends, the contributor walks away with her head held high.

Scientific studies have shown that effective listening by the leader can improve the performance of contributors. In many organizations, however, managers and executives do not listen well, even to their peers. One study of 275 executives on twenty-six top corporate teams found good listening to be in short supply: "There was, instead, frequent inattention, many interruptions, and almost reflexive arguing and counterarguing, much of which failed to address the issues, and nearly all of which simply reinforced existing opinions."[3] But most are capable of learning good listening skills. After coaching, one top executive remarked, "I never realized what keeping my mouth shut would accomplish. I'm hearing things now I never would've heard before."[4]

Interpersonal Listening

Who has the best ideas for improving performance in your organization? The answer is that every person has potentially good ideas — which is why leaders need to listen. Listening is one of the organization's most powerful tools, because the people doing the work have the most experience and insight into improving both how the work is done and how it is planned and managed.

Like many executives, John was an introvert, somewhat shy. His knowledge and organizational leadership skills got him promoted to vice president and site manager of a large electronics assembly plant. Though not by nature a good listener, he did talk frequently with his workers. One of his manufacturing work teams improved their on-time delivery of products from 90 percent to 99 percent.

The team invited John to the work area to hear them talk about how they improved their performance. John listened and grew excited about how the results were going to translate into profit; he was impressed by team members' enthusiasm and pride in their ideas, and by how well the ideas worked.

After the meeting and in the days that followed, John asked individual team members for more details of their creative ideas. As they spoke, he listened attentively, and they grew even more enthusiastic about improving quality, productivity, and efficiency in all their work processes. John discovered that he enjoyed listening to his contributors, who were focused on goals similar to his own — improving performance.

Great interpersonal leaders are not necessarily the most gregarious of people; they are just leaders who take the time to listen to people. One leader I knew would go to each contributor's desk at least once a day, ostensibly to drop off some document or ask a question. Actually, he was creating an opportunity for each person to interact, perhaps to share an idea. Tom Peters and Bob Waterman (*In Search of Excellence*) saw the same behavior in leaders of top-performing companies and shared a memorable phrase: "management by wandering around."

Checking Understanding

Hearing is not the same as listening. Both leaders and contributors sometimes tend to dominate a conversation.

Whether leader or contributor, the listener who is thinking about a counterargument, considering how to word a reply, or preoccupied with other concerns can easily miss important parts of what is being said. A major principle of Side by Side Leadership is that communication is interactive, not one-way lecturing. That is why a good Side by Side leader or contributor not only takes care to focus her attention on the contributor's words, but checks her understanding afterward — simply by summarizing or paraphrasing what the speaker has just said. This turns a one-way conversation into two-way communication.

Albert Einstein was noted for his informal, interactive way of searching for scientific truth. As intelligent as he was, he never assumed that he understood what others told him; he checked his understanding not only of what people

THE MOST HELPFUL INTERPERSONAL LEADERS NOT ONLY LISTEN NONJUDGMENTALLY BUT ARE NON JUDGMENTAL WHEN THEY CHECK UNDERSTANDING. IT IS IMPORTANT TO CHECK UNDERSTANDING-

- WHEN PEOPLE ARE ARGUING,
- WHEN SOMEONE IS SHARING A PROBLEM,
- WHEN SOMEONE IS ASKING THE LEADER TO PERFORM A TASK, OR
- WHEN TALKING WITH SOMEONE FROM A DIFFERENT CULTURE OR FOR WHOM ENGLISH IS THE SECOND LANGUAGE.

said but of the questions they asked. One reason he was so widely respected was that he showed respect for all who spoke with him.

It is important to check understanding when someone is requesting or delegating action. The listener needs to verify the exact goals, the level of detail needed, and the work required to accomplish the goal.

Listening and checking understanding are hard work, requiring well-developed powers of concentration. Psychologist

Robert Carkhuff once remarked that no one could be a good counselor unless he could run one mile without stopping. He believed that the stamina and concentration of a dedicated runner were similar to those needed to be a good listener.

Skill 8: Mutual Contributing

In 1927 Charles Lindbergh entered an international competition to complete the first nonstop solo transatlantic flight from New York to Paris. He knew that his airplane, the *Spirit of St. Louis,* had to be built as quickly as possible if he was to win the competition and secure his place in aviation history.

Lindbergh traveled to Ryan Aeronautical Company in San Diego, where his airplane was being assembled, and offered to help. He soon noticed that at intervals throughout the day, the workers would stop assembling the plane and sweep the hangar floor to keep dirt and debris from getting into the airplane or its engine. One time, after the assemblers went back to work on the plane, Lindbergh picked up a broom and made it his task to keep the floor clean so they would not have to stop.

Even though he helped design the plane and was to be its pilot, Lindbergh pitched in and did whatever was necessary to help others stay on schedule toward the goal. With his help, Ryan built Lindbergh's airplane in record time, and Lindbergh flew into history by crossing the Atlantic Ocean on May 2, 1927.

Being an outstanding contributor is one way that you can acquire the power to influence others: when you contribute selflessly, people give you the power. When someone gives you a task to perform, he is giving you a little bit of power.

There are three ways leaders can increase their power by being contributors:

1. Perform any task they are assigned with excellence and enthusiasm.

2. Be a willing contributor for other leaders (and subordinates, too).

3. Uphold the values of the organization.

Perform tasks cheerfully and well. Scientists and engineers at Bell Labs invented many of the devices that support today's instantaneous worldwide communication. Robert Kelly found that a primary difference between these "superstars" and less illustrious peers was their networking.[5] They formed key relationships with the organization's movers and shakers by rapidly completing assigned tasks and going beyond what was expected. They were great team workers, took initiative, and did high-priority work; they also performed quickly and competently any task their leaders asked of them, no matter how unimportant it seemed.

Contribute willingly. Another way leaders can be contributors is by helping other leaders. In any eight-hour day, leaders find themselves following instructions and completing work needed by contributors, executives, or other leaders. Even the top executive must follow priorities set by the board of directors, by regulators, and by customers. By contributing what is asked of him promptly and flawlessly, the leader models the contributor skills he wants others to practice.

Uphold the organization's values. Contributors are more supportive of leaders who abide by the organization's norms and values. The late Sam Walton, founder of discount giant Wal-Mart, spent four days a week visiting his stores throughout North America. He would give a speech to employees, then visit with customers. He was modeling behavior he expected of all his executives: get into the field and stay in touch with employees and customers.

You can be a leader in your organization by contributing to an important goal that someone else has set and by working in harmony with your organization's values. Look for opportunities to help others achieve their goals, even if it means you sometimes get to sweep the floor.

Look for opportunities to help others achieve their goals, even if it means you sometimes get to sweep the floor.

Skill 9: Connecting Visionary Goals

Why are some leaders so easy to follow? What special quality draws people to them? In a word, charisma, an attribute that many people consider innate rather than learned. Although it is true that some people seem born with the ability to connect with others, anyone can learn to be more charismatic and to motivate contributors by connecting with the hopes and dreams of others.

In the best-performing organizations, charismatic leaders at all levels, not just at the top, create teams that achieve high levels of performance.[6] They communicate goals and actions in a way that energizes both leaders and contributors. This excitement generates large volumes of high-quality work from motivated people, who willingly work longer hours. The leader's charisma influences contributors' satisfaction with their work and their commitment to the organization.

If you can honestly connect your own values with the audience's values, you'll create energy.

Charisma can be contagious. When retail store managers communicate a positive attitude, their workers interact well with each other and with customers. This boosts the store's sales performance and shrinks turnover.[7] Success and goodwill follow naturally.

Motivating contributors often begins with a speech by the leader. Remember, the main thing you want to do is build a connection between your values and goals and those of your listeners. Before you speak to a large audience, discover their goals and what's important to them in relation to what you are presenting. If you can honestly connect your own values with the audience's values, you'll create energy.

Every accomplished public speaker knows that body language is an important component of the message. Your facial expression should support your words. Don't smile when you're discussing serious matters. If you're talking about the team's most important goal, get some excitement into your voice. But if you fail to relate your goals with those of your audience, or if you are not sincerely interested in their values, your audience will pick up on it and you will fail to move them. You may speak strongly and create a dramatic impression, but people will see your body language as showmanship rather than sincere passion; you will not generate charisma.

To motivate people, express optimism; use positive language. Don't say, "You're doing a lousy job this month." Instead, say, "Let's look at that phenomenal month we had last year and see what we were doing right." The winner of the U.S. presidential election can often be predicted on the basis of who uses the most positive language and wages the most positive campaign. Ronald Reagan was a master at telling voters his vision of a great future and avoiding negative campaigning.[8]

Sometimes, of course, the negatives are unavoidable. When problems must be discussed, talk of them as challenges that will be overcome, not as eternal troubles. In their book *The Charismatic Factor,* Robert Richardson and Katherine Thayer write, "Optimistic leaders never discuss difficulties in permanent terms but always in finite terms."[9] People who stay highly motivated in their daily lives think this way. U.S. Secretary of State Colin Powell keeps this motto close at hand: "Perpetual optimism is a force multiplier."

Skill 10: Diverse Networking

Think back on your career. What were your best jobs? How did you get them? If you're like most people, you learned of some of your best opportunities through friends, colleagues, or family members, by simple word of mouth. I found ten of my first twelve jobs this way — through networking.

Networking doesn't stop just because you get hired; on the job is where it shows its full value. The Side by Side leader, whose core principle is the two-way interaction, falls naturally into networking. A leader with strong interpersonal skills almost always communicates with a wide-ranging, informal network of friends, acquaintances, colleagues, mentors, professionals in other industries, and experts in various fields who can help the leader progress toward his goals — and whom the leader helps in similar ways whenever he sees an opportunity. Successful leaders do favors for people in their network and keep them informed of their own successes.[10] The unwritten rule is that everyone in the network gives without expecting anything in return.

When he was CEO of Chase Manhattan Bank, David Rockefeller kept a record of every person he met, what was discussed, and favors that were exchanged. He had thousands of names in files organized by geographic region and affiliation. When he planned a trip, he reviewed the summary sheets on his past contacts and acquaintances in the cities he was visiting, and he invited them to social gatherings. David Rockefeller used his informal network to solicit, screen, and facilitate multimillion-dollar bank loans to leaders of other companies and countries.

For the most effective networking, keep a positive attitude. When someone calls or comes to see you, view it not as an interruption but as an opportunity. Use the interaction to strengthen your network by helping the other person. Networking is give and take: give help now, and one day your network will help you achieve your goals.

Banking on Knowledge

The intellectual capital available through an extended network helps create new intellectual capital. Knowledge is shared and discussed on the telephone, by e-mail, and face-to-face. Linus Pauling, Albert Einstein, and other great scientists networked with knowledge leaders inside and outside their fields. David Rockefeller's networks included many important organizational and political knowledge leaders. Venture capitalists place great value on entrepreneurial and management teams with successful track records and specialized knowledge.

Of particular value is the kind of intellectual capital — scientific discoveries, technological breakthroughs, new-product business plans — that is not generally available outside the network. In a healthy network, such information becomes readily accessible for problem solving because members trust each other to be honest and not take unfair advantage.

Developing Talent

Leaders with the best networks typically began forming them as students. They added professors whose knowledge and wisdom guided them, fellow students of exceptional talent, people they met on their first jobs, even experts in seemingly unrelated fields. Sometimes the network grew to include a high-level manager who became a mentor. People who have had the benefit of mentoring based on shared goals often achieve early career success.[11]

The most effective leaders select several star subordinates to coach and develop. They get together informally with their protégés every few days and share information in an open, Side by Side dialogue. Effective leaders get out of the office and casually drop in to see their contributors, giving them an opportunity to voice concerns or share ideas.[12]

Strength in Diversity

One key attribute of the most effective networks is diversity. Research has shown that engineers, scientists, marketing experts, and other knowledge leaders are more productive, creative, and knowledgeable when they have a variety of relationships both inside and outside the organization.[13] With access to more data sources in different fields, leaders who develop a diverse network gain a creative edge over those whose network includes only people like themselves. Every network is unique, and each relationship in a natural network is unique.

Effective team and organizational leaders develop relationships with customers, suppliers, competitors, bankers, stockholders, and other outsiders in the natural course of events. They use both formal and informal approaches. These strong interpersonal leaders are active in their trade associations for intra-industry contacts and in their local chambers of commerce for inter-industry relationships. People who network with only their own interests in mind usually fail; the people who are being exploited quickly sense that the relationship is self-serving, not reciprocal.

Prepare to Share

The main purpose of Side by Side networking is for leaders to help each other achieve their visionary goals. Strong interpersonal leaders ask questions to learn their colleagues' values and visionary goals, then send them information and referrals that will help them achieve those goals — articles, books, business opportunities, people and organizations to contact.

Top networkers meet their fellow networkers frequently to stay in touch and up-to-date. Television personality Bryant Gumbel writes one personal note a day to someone in his network or someone he wishes to congratulate or thank. A real estate executive invites network colleagues to gather on holidays. Yet another networker I admire talks to forty or fifty people a day by telephone, one or two minutes each. Regular two-way communication is how Side by Side leaders keep their networking relationships alive and healthy.

Chapter 15

Sphere 4:

Team Leadership

Leading by Mutually Managing Team Interactions, Goals, Skills, Roles, and Capabilities

A team is a group, but a group is not a team. Most work groups are "teams" in name only. Their members typically come to the first meeting with no idea of why they were chosen or what the meeting is about. They sit silently as one or two managers talk about an issue or a problem. They may be asked for information, but rarely an opinion. They are not asked to make any decisions, set any goals, or come up with any new ideas. They are told how to fix the problem or resolve the issue, after which the meeting is adjourned.

Most such "teams" fail to achieve significant results. In fact, they do not operate as a real team in any way. "Group" is the only word that accurately conveys their makeup and functioning. And yet, over the past ten years, I have watched real teams produce outstanding results. These were not teams in name only, but teams that were structured and trained to function as teams in reality.

What do we mean by "group," and what do we mean by "team"? The table on the next page outlines the essential differences between the two concepts. Team leaders who used the "structured team" formula produced results that were in most cases far superior to those of "groups."

Group	Structured Team	Vital Differences
Begins with no clear purpose.	Leader begins with written charter identifying areas of improvement or focus that will help whole organization.	The team charter is like a compass that directs the team on its journey.
People are assigned to group with little thought.	Members are selected whose work, if better coordinated, would be more productive.	Improved coordination among team members reduces duplication, waste, costs; boosts productivity, quality.
Does not develop its own goals.	Team & leader develop specific team goals and measures.	Team goals connect members' goals & actions; together they support organization's goals.
No new or creative strategies, action steps, solutions, goals, or structured creativity.	Leader & members are trained in team creativity skills that are used to develop creative strategies for achieving team goals.	Team creativity is responsible for ideas that improve performance 30–300%. Team is proactive, not just reactive.
Roles undefined.	Members develop roles, action plans to achieve goals.	Defined roles, action plans rapidly implement creative ideas.
Does not make decisions, or takes too long to decide.	Team is taught decision-making skills, uses matrix showing decisions that can be made as team or by individuals.	Team members together or as individuals can solve problems, implement work improvements, make decisions without waiting for management approval.
No group meetings, or people present only information.	Leader ensures team meetings are used to reach goals, solve problems, make decisions, improve key work processes.	Without team meetings, people will waste 5–8 hours a week in random communication trying to meet needs that a one-hour team meeting could achieve.
No written work processes or "playbook."	Key work processes are written down, streamlined, continuously improved.	Team excels by continuously improving its work processes.
No group training.	Leader ensures team receives continuous training in team, technical skills.	With additional knowledge, team makes better decisions, improves work processes.

The more I worked with teams and organizations, and the more I looked at the research, the clearer the concept of "team" became to me. "Teamwork" is more than simply getting along with and helping one another out; it actually involves five identifiable behavioral components. Because each can be labeled with a word beginning with the letter C, I call these behaviors "C^5 teamwork," as in "C to the fifth power."

Side by Side leaders, trained in the skills of listening and power sharing, find it natural to create and work in C^5 teams — teams that have achieved all five of the levels of

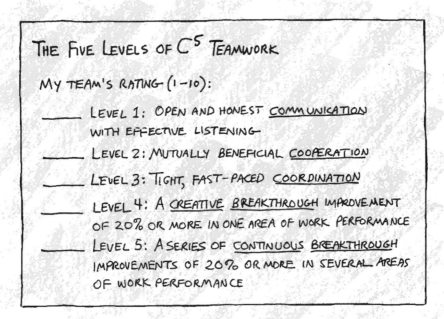

THE FIVE LEVELS OF C^5 TEAMWORK

MY TEAM'S RATING (1-10):

_____ LEVEL 1: OPEN AND HONEST COMMUNICATION WITH EFFECTIVE LISTENING

_____ LEVEL 2: MUTUALLY BENEFICIAL COOPERATION

_____ LEVEL 3: TIGHT, FAST-PACED COORDINATION

_____ LEVEL 4: A CREATIVE BREAKTHROUGH IMPROVEMENT OF 20% OR MORE IN ONE AREA OF WORK PERFORMANCE

_____ LEVEL 5: A SERIES OF CONTINUOUS BREAKTHROUGH IMPROVEMENTS OF 20% OR MORE IN SEVERAL AREAS OF WORK PERFORMANCE

teamwork shown here. Of the more than 100 teams I have asked to use this scale to evaluate their own teamwork, most rate themselves at level 1 or 2.

Try rating a team you are on in all five areas. Score 1 if your team is very low in an area, 10 if very high.

When team leaders in a wide range of organizations — from high-tech companies to nonprofits — helped their teams develop C^5 teamwork, they created new wealth. At Advanced Micro Devices' Submicron Development Center in Sunnyvale, California, eighty-four teams achieved $50 million in documented improvements by developing structured teams. Here are the five most important team leadership skills that these team leaders used to achieve multimillion-dollar results:

Skill 11: Managing the interface

Skill 12: Setting team goals

Skill 13: Using structured team skills

Skill 14: Coordinating team roles

Skill 15: Increasing team capacity

Skill 11: Managing the Interface

Side by Side team leaders are skillful at facilitating interactions between the team and outside interaction fields. This is a very important skill, because great teamwork begins and ends outside the team. The success of the team is graded by people outside the team and is based on how well the team makes improvements and achieves goals that are linked to the organization's visionary goals.

INDIVIDUAL CONTRIBUTOR'S GOAL

In one organization, two leaders (we'll call them "Dan" and "Alice") were appointed to lead two different research teams. The company's sales had been slipping for years, but the research department had developed a new product that the company's visionary president believed would boost sales well into the next decade. Dan's team was assigned to develop a marketing plan; Alice's team was charged with resolving several production problems.

At the initial meeting between Dan, Alice, and the president, Dan asked very few questions. Based on his many years of experience with other organizations, he was confident that he could quickly develop a marketing plan. After the meeting, he assembled his team and gave directions.

Alice, on the other hand, was full of questions. She had so many questions that the president became slightly irritated. Before meeting with her team, she talked with other managers in the organization, getting information on the company's values, visionary goals, and annual goals, and how they affected her project. As her team worked on solutions to the production problems, she visited the president and other managers to

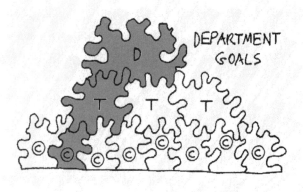

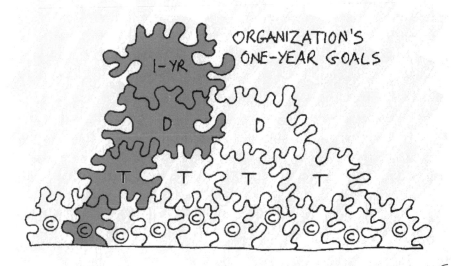

see how the team's work meshed with the company's other projects and goals.

One week before the new product's scheduled launch, Alice and Dan addressed a large meeting of the company's senior management. Alice gave details of the production problems and how they had been overcome. She was asked only a few questions, because she had kept management informed of her team's progress. Although some problems

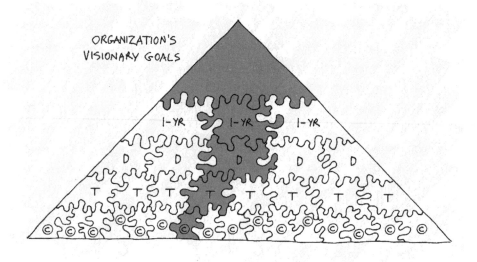

remained, everyone in the company was aware of them and knew progress was being made toward resolving them.

Then it was Dan's turn. He detailed his marketing plan, which was based on concepts and goals he had learned from other organizations. He believed that his plan would be an effective way to market the new product. When he finished his talk, the room was silent. Unfortunately, it wasn't because they were struck speechless by his brilliance. It was because everyone except Dan realized that his approach did not fit the priorities of the company.

Alice had worked behind the scenes, as well as in team meetings, to promote the team's support of her department's and organization's annual and long-range visionary goals. In a Side by Side–led organization, the goals fit together at every level. For a team to operate successfully within a visionary goal–led organization, the team leader must ensure that the team's goals support those of the organization — because great teamwork begins and ends outside the team.

The Team Charter

Research shows that one of the best ways to align teams with the organization's goals is by means of a team charter. Group members who were not given clear expectations and role definitions took as long as eighteen months to begin acting effectively as a team, while teams that worked out team charters with their leaders began to see improved results within a month.

A team charter is an informal document that specifies the structure, purpose, and scope of the team, the importance of the problem to be solved or process to be improved, and a chronology of recent key events. It covers the organizational goals that the team will affect; names of team members; available resources; decision-making authority; and the team's start date and anticipated completion date. Later, the team will develop its own goals and goal measures to carry out the charter.

TEAM CHARTER

TEAM SPONSOR:

USEFUL BACKGROUND INFORMATION:

BUSINESS AREAS THE TEAM WILL IMPACT:

TEAM DECISION-MAKING POWER:

    TEAM WILL DECIDE:

    TEAM WILL ONLY RECOMMEND THE FOLLOWING
        DECISIONS (TO WHOM):

TEAM MEMBERS:

TEAM LEADER:

OTHER RESOURCES:

START DATE:

ANTICIPATED COMPLETION DATE:

The team leader and team sponsor usually work side by side preparing the first draft of the charter. The team sponsor is the executive, manager, or contributor who "owns" the goals, problems, or processes the team is chartered to improve. Duties of the team sponsor include approving the time, money, and other resources the team will need; promoting the team and its efforts; removing barriers; determining accountability; and recognizing and rewarding achievement.

Team leaders sometimes make the mistake of walking into the first meeting with the team charter in hand and saying, "This is what the boss wants, so that's what we're going to do." A better first-meeting approach is a team discussion with the sponsor, in which team members, leader, and sponsor are encouraged to comment and propose changes to the charter. Depending on the number of changes proposed and discussed, the team and sponsor can usually agree on a charter within the hour.

Once the team charter is established, everyone, including the team sponsor, must comply with it if the team is to work effectively. Although it is an informal document, it records the team leader's and sponsor's support of each team member's role in making decisions and achieving goals. The charter can be revised, but a Side by Side approach should be used in that case as well.

With the team charter in place, the team leader should protect the team against undue interference from above or outside. He should make sure the team meets at regular times and that its members get all the time and information they need to achieve the team goals. Team members should get training in the team skills needed for generating ideas, holding meetings, solving problems, and reaching goals.

MANGAGING OTHER INTERFACES

SIDE BY SIDE TEAM LEADERS ASSIST THE TEAM BY PROVIDING 3 INGREDIENTS:

• RESOURCES (INCLUDING TIME)

• INFORMATION

• SKILLS OR LEARNING

Having completed team skills training, the members of one computer chip manufacturing team were ready to pursue team goals, but their leader, under pressure from the overall production manager, told the team not to meet for the next six weeks. The company, they were told, had to quickly increase production to meet rising demand, and the meetings would cut into the team's productivity.

Another team in the same department, however, continued to meet after their training. Their leader protected them from interference; he believed that his team could accomplish their goals and still keep productivity high. They continued tracking their progress, solving problems, and working toward their goals. Some members worked away from their assigned manufacturing positions in order to complete team tasks.

At the end of six weeks, the second team was way ahead of the first in productivity. Somehow, the team members who took time off the line to pursue team goals actually got more work done. The weekly team meetings led to daily improvements that increased productivity in the long run.

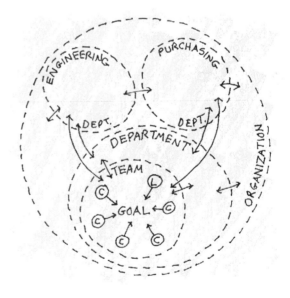

Teams are not islands; they are part of their departments and part of the company as a whole. When teams agree on goals that support the goals in these larger interaction fields, productivity rises. Team leaders must also work with the interaction fields of other departments to ensure the team's success. A manufacturing team needs to work with engineering, purchasing, and human resources, among other fields. By understanding the interaction fields that affect the team, the leader can win support for the team's efforts while coordinating its activities with those of other teams. The best business improvements come from combined, coordinated thinking toward goals shared by cross-functional teams of people across the company's interaction fields.

Skill 12: Setting Team Goals

Goal setting is one of the most powerful motivators in the workplace. I've watched team members who couldn't care less suddenly become committed workers when their Side by Side team leader helped them set reach-out goals. Team members who are allowed to set goals, check progress, and develop and track action plans perform 30 to 70 percent better than their nonempowered peers.[1] In the field of engineering, the number-one predictor of success in research and development teams is the quality of team involvement and communication in developing project goals.[2]

Even though a group may be called a team, it is not truly a team until it sets and works toward shared team goals. Team goals are short term (3 to 6 months) and describe specifically what needs to be achieved in what time frame. They should be written according to the STAR formula — that is, team goals should be

- **S**pecific (stated in specific, observable terms)
- **T**ime-based (target date for completion no longer than six months out)
- **A**ligned (supporting the organization's visionary goals)
- **R**each-out (challenging but possible)

Team goals, although inspiring by nature, cannot be achieved if management or the work team goes on with business as usual; the team must immediately brainstorm ways to measure and track their achievement. Goal measures that are easy to gather data on are hard to develop. Creating good goal measures usually requires the full creative effort of the entire team.

Setting team goals will not in and of itself dramatically improve productivity. It takes a full package deal of team structures and team skills to come up with creative strategies, breakthrough solutions, and improved, simplified work processes.

Skill 13: Using Structured Team Skills

Teams that achieve outstanding productivity have leaders who model structured team skills and processes and hold the team accountable for using them. These skills and processes produce many benefits: commitment and ownership by team members, and a positive work environment that increases motivation and creativity. Problem-solving teams that used a similar structured problem-solving model improved productivity in an aluminum manufacturing plant as well as in numerous computer chip factories. Following a structured process to make team decisions resulted in superior decisions.[3]

In 1993, Advanced Micro Devices trained nine teams in structured team skills. Each team spent thirty-two hours learning and applying team skills to their work. In less than one year, while team training was still under way, the nine teams averaged nearly $1 million each in savings.

> TO REALIZE OPTIMUM TEAM PERFORMANCE, THE TEAM LEADER MUST
>
> - ENSURE THAT THE TEAM IS TRAINED IN STRUCTURED TEAM SKILLS FOR SHARED SELF-MANAGEMENT,
>
> - ENCOURAGE THE USE OF STRUCTURED TEAM SKILLS IN ALL THE TEAM'S WORK AND MEETINGS, AND
>
> - MODEL TEAM SKILLS IN ALL INTERACTIONS.

Structured Team Skills

While reviewing more than 1,200 research studies, I identified the ten key structures that team leaders can use to achieve C^5 teamwork. They represent the team skills that breakthrough teams consistently use as they do their work. Although there's a more complete discussion of these team structures in my previous book *Breakthrough Teamwork,* the table on the next page summarizes the ten components of structured teamwork and how they benefit teams and team members.

Stanford University professor Kathleen Eisenhardt researched team creativity in high-tech companies. Among eight Silicon Valley microcomputer firms in the study, those whose management teams considered many alternative solutions simultaneously were the most successful.[4]

Skill 14: Coordinating Team Roles

If team roles and responsibilities are properly designed, everybody's work blends together to achieve the team's goals; if they are not, some things don't get done properly, or on time, or at all, while other efforts may be duplicated. For this reason, after setting team goals, the team should immediately specify each member's role in the team's daily work and responsibility for completion of tasks.

Most of the several hundred teams my colleagues and I have worked with took off like a rocket after the roles and responsibilities were developed. The Side by Side team method is to have each team member and the team leader write a first draft of his role and responsibilities. Along with his job duties, he should list the tasks he shares with other team members. Working as a team member should be considered a normal part of his job, not something extra. Each team member, including the leader, then presents his draft to the whole team for questions and revisions. Any subsequent changes are made by consensus.

Occasionally, the team may be held back by one member's poor performance. When this happens, the team leader can sit down with him and explore remedies in a two-way, Side by Side discussion (chapter 2). Letting the team member speak first often leads to a faster solution to the problem.

Another structured team process that is useful is to identify important tasks and track progress in those areas toward achieving the team's goals. The Gantt chart, invented

Team Structures	How They Benefit Teams
Team creativity to promote breakthrough	Use structured creativity skills to encourage all to participate. Team creativity is the key to achieving breakthrough results.
Ground rules, norms to build open communication & trust	Supportive work climate promotes creativity, breakthrough thinking, risk taking, team member commitment, and effective team communication.
Team mission to unify the idealism	These establish work priorities, unleash idealism, align the team with the organization's vision, mission, goals.
Setting of team goals to bring breakthrough	Effective team goal setting and action planning promote team member involvement, commitment, motivation.
Meetings to coordinate breakthrough improvements	Team meeting skills & structures harness the energy of group dynamics, bring high goal achievement. Establishing high-performance/commitment team meetings produces high-performance/commitment culture; energy contagious.
Team responsibilities & decision matrix to coordinate empowered decision making, action	Roles & responsibilities are established & clarified regarding how each team member supports the other team members, the team's linkages to internal & external customers. Teams know who has authority to make what decisions.
Conflict management controls differences	When employees are asked to bring their hearts & minds to work, to care & think about quality, productivity, & cycle time reduction, there are conflicts — which can be healthy & result in breakthrough solutions when team members have effective conflict management skills.
Team problem solving to respond to big & small crises	Team members enthusiastically assume role of solving problems together in & out of team meetings vs. bumping them up to management & griping. Using basic, easy-to-implement problem-solving steps, team members solve problems in team meetings & on the fly as they work.
Team decision making to make good decisions rapidly	These skills required for most difficult of all team participative management tasks: decision making. Without them, teams flounder, waste time, get in arguments, end up with manager making the decision. With them, teams make better decisions, experience high commitment, rapid decision implementation.
Work process improvement to improve the team's playbook	Team members learn how to improve work processes. Work in all organizations undergoes bureaucratic creep, with process steps losing value they once had. Team members look for ways to improve work processes, eliminate waste, & cut cycle time.

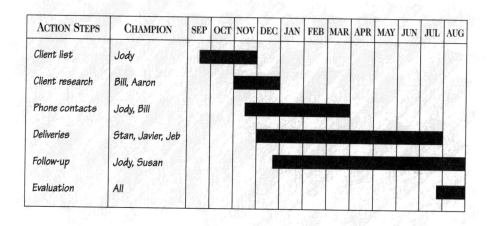

ACTION STEPS	CHAMPION	SEP	OCT	NOV	DEC	JAN	FEB	MAR	APR	MAY	JUN	JUL	AUG
Client list	Jody	███											
Client research	Bill, Aaron		███										
Phone contacts	Jody, Bill				████████								
Deliveries	Stan, Javier, Jeb					███████████████							
Follow-up	Jody, Susan						████████████						
Evaluation	All												██

by Henry Gantt, is an excellent and widely used tool for this purpose. It is basically a graphic showing the start and completion times for each essential task. It has three major elements: action steps, the "champion" or persons responsible for seeing that the action is completed, and the timeline for each action step. Every team member should participate in identifying action steps, champions, and timelines. Structured creativity is often the best way to accomplish this, because hearing every voice is the best way to ensure that no essential steps are overlooked. Team leaders have a special responsibility to hold team members accountable between meetings — for example, by making sure they complete assignments before the next meeting.

Regular Team Meetings

There's a proven tool the team leader can use to track and coordinate the team's work — the regular team meeting. By reviewing measures and action plans, team members become aware of obstacles to their progress. Those that the team cannot handle alone are automatically the leader's responsibility.

Measuring and acknowledging team members' progress toward goals boosts performance. In one organization, providing visual, public feedback daily on quality goals brought a 66 percent drop in rework.[5] In another study, feedback combined with team goal setting raised productivity 75 percent.[6]

Not too long ago, as I was training some managers in Side by Side team leadership skills, one manager said, "I had a team that set wonderful goals. They developed goal measures and even a great action plan. I was so excited! But they never reached their goals. It turned out to be a waste of time."

"Did they track their action items and action plan at regular team meetings?" I asked.

He slumped in his chair. "No, they didn't." And understanding dawned on his face.

Remember that a Side by Side team leader leads both during and between team meetings, nurturing members, sharing successes and concerns. When a team member has accepted an assignment, the leader tracks her progress between meetings, provides encouragement and accountability, and finds solutions to obstacles in her path to success.

Skill 15: Increasing Team Capacity

The Side by Side leader expands his team's capability and resources by looking for opportunities to help his team members grow. He makes sure the team receives the best available technical knowledge and skills training because, as research shows, teams that get team skills training perform better, participate better, and work better independently when the team leader is not there.

You have personal goals. I have personal goals. The same is true of team members. Team members' interests and personal goals can form the basis for their particular task assignments and responsibilities. The best leaders talk with team members to discover and support their personal values and interests; by doing so, they make their people more productive, and their goals an asset to the team.[7]

Team leaders need to be able to coach. Side by Side leaders coach team and technical skills by observing how team members perform their work and then working beside them to improve their mastery of their skills.

As you grow in Side by Side team leadership, look for ways to balance your ideas with the ideas of your contributors — your fellow team members. When you work side by side with them, together you accomplish amazing things.

Chapter 16

Sphere 5:

Organizational Leadership

Leading by Seeking Opportunities, Values, Visionary Goals, Creative Strategies, and Flexibility

The executives at Vastar Resources, a subsidiary of Atlantic Richfield Oil Company, were frustrated. Their company had been spun out of ARCO a few years back with a successful IPO. Its performance, however, was stuck in the bottom half of its competition group of large-capitalization, independent oil and gas companies (chapter 7).

The Vastar executives knew they had to change the company's culture. It would take more than the ideas top management alone could come up with. The CEO and seven vice presidents named forty-two key employees to join their leadership team. Together they formed the nucleus of an expanded leadership group that became known as "Team 50." The team developed a vision for the organization: to become the premier exploration and production company in the oil and gas industry.

Team 50 began instilling a new culture, using the five Side by Side organizational leadership skills:

Skill 16: Identifying opportunities and threats. Team 50 collected and summarized all available data and knowledge on the current opportunities and threats, both internal and external, to achieving their business success. All levels of the organization were involved in this effort.

Skill 17: Living organizational values. The team held open meetings at all levels to identify and develop the organization's values and vision, in relation to both the company's goals and outside influences.

Skill 18: Setting organizational visionary goals. With input from all personnel, Team 50 set measurable visionary goals that were 200 percent higher than current performance.

Skill 19: Creating new strategies. Team 50 leaders met with all of their employees to develop new strategies and action plans to achieve the visionary goals.

Skill 20: Creating a flexible organization. Vastar's leaders formed strategic alliances with key organizations that could help them reach their visionary goals, and used empowered teams both inside and outside the company.

Vastar applied these five skills to create its "Breakthrough Culture." Every employee was a member of a team that set visionary goals for its work group, developed creative strategies to achieve its goals, and was empowered to rapidly implement its own ideas for improvement. The company formed a variety of cross-organizational teams to achieve important goals, such as improving technology, reducing the time and cost of locating and recovering oil and gas, and creating new kinds of compensation and performance incentives.

By the end of 1997, two years after implementing these Side by Side Leadership processes, Vastar became one of the top three companies in its competition group and was number one in 1998 in shareholder return. Two years later, British Petroleum, which had previously merged with ARCO, bought the publicly held stock of Vastar for $83 per share. The market value of Vastar had increased $5.5 billion in six years — a 300 percent return to shareholders — during a period of low oil and gas prices and intense competition.

Would you like to achieve a 300 percent performance improvement in your company? The five Side by Side organizational leadership skills will smooth the way. But it's a package deal; the skills are part of a unified strategy. Using one or two or three of them won't get you the breakthrough performance you want. They work together; use them all.

Skill 16: Identifying Opportunities & Threats

If you lead an organization, should your main concerns be what's happening inside, with your employees and their work results, or outside, with your customers and competitors? I believe the answer is both. Leaders get the best results by looking simultaneously inside and outside the organization and applying their organizational leadership skills wherever they will help the most in achieving the organization's goals.

Leaders who believe in the value of rapid response take care to learn of business opportunities and dangers from people both inside and outside the organization.

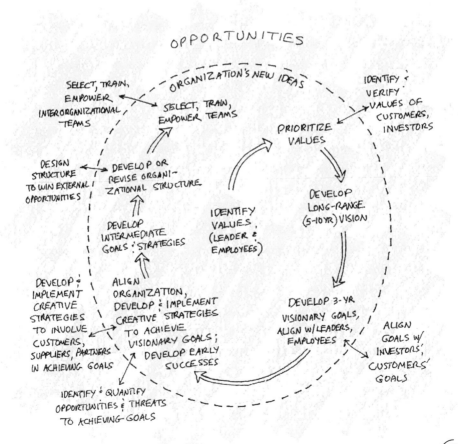

When Andy Grove was CEO of Intel (chapter 12), he made it known that he would welcome e-mail from anyone in the organization, especially when it concerned a potential opportunity or a threat to the business. His only request was that the sender back up a suggestion with the best available data. By inviting input and listening, he created an organizational culture that encouraged people to find and share information.

First rule of organizational breakthrough: There must be pressure for change or there will be no change.

Side by Side organizational leaders network with people from various departments as well as people from a wide range of other organizations. They attend trade association meetings and chamber of commerce gatherings to collect vital information on what is happening outside their organization.

Much of the pressure for change comes from global competition, not just for customers but for new technologies, equipment, and suppliers that are becoming available to all, including end consumers. As you read trade magazines and newspaper articles and talk with people both inside and outside your organization, what do you discover that points to a need for change?

Here's the first rule of organizational breakthrough: There must be pressure for change or there will be no breakthrough. Both research and experience tell us that being aware of external and internal pressures for major change is a huge factor in achieving success. Effective leaders use crises to kick-start major changes. The emotions that surface during a crisis can be harnessed to get things moving.

Skill 17: Living Organizational Values

James Collins and Jerry Porras found that companies that take their organization's values seriously — among them IBM, Hewlett-Packard, and Sony — had 600 percent higher stock value, as well as greater job security and more opportunities for job growth and learning, than the companies they were compared with.[1] The successful companies were also the ones that diligently followed their core values, some of which, as with GE and Merck, had not changed in over seventy years.

Although their organizations' values may be old, Side by Side leaders always look for ways to freshen and revitalize them. They look outside for new ideas and methods, and inside for people who best uphold and exemplify the values. One organization I worked with, which held teamwork as one of its seven core values, was always on the lookout for new ways to improve the company's already good teamwork.

Value-based organizations maintain high standards and do not compromise them for any reason. (Two of Merck's core values are to advance medical science and to serve humanity.) People who do not uphold the standards are, at a minimum, made to feel uncomfortable and asked to improve. Under CEO Jack Welch, General Electric offers a second chance to any manager whose performance suffers, but people who violate GE's values are immediately shown the door.

People prefer working for a company that promotes strong core values and bases all activities, systems, and behaviors on them. In 1996, some Advanced Micro Devices technicians left to work at other Austin chip factories, but later returned, sometimes at lower salaries, because they liked working in AMD's team culture.

Values Inside and Out

Strong organizational values should be based on the values of three associated groups: customers, employees, and shareholders (or stakeholders). The values that everyone can agree on — where the three groups overlap — are the strongest and most likely to be shared; they must be upheld by people at all levels of the organization. Professors John Kotter and James Heskett of Harvard found that companies that combined the values of all three groups achieved 700 percent greater profits over eleven years than companies that recognized the values of only one of the groups. Although the relationship is not necessarily one of cause and effect, values that recognize all three groups appear to be correlated with greater success.[2]

What if the values of customers, employees, and stakeholders appear to be in conflict? This was the situation Dennis Maloney faced when he assumed his duties as chief juvenile probation officer in Bend, Oregon. As head of his organization, Dennis was responsible for locking up, sentencing, and managing juvenile delinquents and youths at risk of committing offenses.

During his first weeks on the job, Dennis did exactly what a Side by Side organizational leader should do. He visited with his customers, stakeholders, and employees to get to know them and to learn their values and goals for his department. He discovered the following conflicting values:

- Police and prosecutors wanted the youthful offenders locked up to keep the community safe.

- Parents wanted their teenagers to get treatment and special programs at home.

- Victims wanted to be reimbursed for damaged or stolen property.

- Judges wanted programs that would prevent repeat offenses.

- Youth advocates and public defenders wanted the youths to stay in the community.

- Juvenile probation employees wanted to help the youths and their families.

Dennis Maloney was also a knowledge leader. He knew what to do to change juvenile delinquents into law-abiding citizens. He knew that holding them accountable for their actions, by giving them community service work and making them pay their victims for damages, was effective. He knew that teaching youths practical living and learning skills reduced their criminal and other problem behaviors. It was also clear to Dennis and his employees that the community was entitled to protection from offenders who threatened the safety of the community. Dennis presented the full range of values in discussions with his employees, community leaders, and national youth-at-risk experts. They came up with a plan they called the "Balanced Approach to Juvenile Probation."

The organization adopted three values: accountability, skill development, and community safety. Dennis's yearly goals and budgets reflected these values. Innovative programs were developed that addressed all three values simultaneously and answered the concerns of customers, employees, and stakeholders. Their success gained state and national recognition. The "Balanced Approach" was made part of the curriculum for training new juvenile judges throughout the United States.[3]

Skill 18: Setting Organizational Visionary Goals

I've noticed, as I suspect you have, that most organizations have vision and mission statements. Do you know the ones for your organization? Vision and mission statements are intended to address these questions:

- Vision: Where are we headed? What will we become in the next five to twenty years?

- Mission: What is our focus for the next three to five years, and what is the idealistic purpose of our focus?

By themselves, vision and mission statements do not create wealth or significantly improve performance. If they did, most organizations with vision and mission statements would be very successful. Unfortunately, most people don't remember them because they are too long — so how can they work day after day to achieve them? Mission and vision statements are useful, however, because they provide a vision of a future toward which people can work.

Visionary goals provide the emotional pull that leads the organization to change and to achieve its mission. They quantify the vision and the mission; that is, they put specific number goals or targets on them — say, for 100 to 300 percent improvement in profits, productivity, or some other measure.

Although visionary goals can lead organizations to great achievements, it doesn't make them easy. In fact, visionary goals should cause most people to say, "That's impossible!" upon first seeing them. And, of course, it *is* impossible, if the only action people take is to work harder doing what they've always done.

In May 1961, President John F. Kennedy proposed a dramatic, seemingly impossible improvement in the performance of the United States. He set a visionary goal: "I believe that this nation should commit itself to achieving the goal, before this decade is out, of landing a man on the moon and returning him safely to the Earth." This specific, reach-out, time-based goal was aligned to both Kennedy's vision and the values of people who supported his New Frontier. At the time, five of the six previous rocket launch attempts had resulted in fiery explosions on the launch pad or shortly after ignition. Many people thought Kennedy's proposal impossible.

Like all great visionary goals, the moon shot energized people. Engineers and technicians worked every day to achieve the necessary intermediate goals, such as developing and launching the huge Saturn rocket. The excitement and teamwork cut across company boundaries. IBM employees shared work with NCR and Honeywell employees to get their part of the job done. On July 20, 1969, the first part of the goal was achieved: *Apollo 11* Astronauts Neil Armstrong and Buzz Aldrin landed on the moon. They completed the mission by safely returning to Earth four days later.

Organizational visionary goals are inspirational. To give everyone in the organization clear focus and challenge, they are usually set three to five years out. They challenge every person and every part of the organization to make the changes necessary to achieve them. As Hamel and Prahalad noted in the *Harvard Business Review*, "This forces the organization to be more inventive to make the most of limited resources."[4]

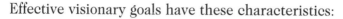

Effective visionary goals have these characteristics:

- They support the overlapping values of customers, stockholders, employees, and other major organizational players.

- They are specific and measurable ways to attain the organization's vision and mission.

- They are so challenging that they force major change in strategies, programs, structure, and everyone's daily work life.

- They have the "Wow!" factor. When people are first told the visionary goal, they say "Wow!"

- They are memorable, to induce people to use them every day to set intermediate goals.

- They are developed by many people, so that the remaining members of the organization buy in fast.

One winter I was working with a nonprofit leadership team who came to the workshop shaking the snow off their overcoats. Their organization was sick. They had seen a significant drop in donations and membership every year for almost four years. Employees were forced into early retirement. Local branch after local branch were closing their doors all over the United States.

The leaders agreed that their organization had no visionary goals. They had long mission statements and vision statements and purpose statements on the walls and in their publications, but no specific, challenging goals. One of my colleagues and I showed the leaders the characteristics of good visionary goals. They challenged us: "Dennis, how do you expect us to set visionary growth goals for our organization when we are dying?" I said, "Trust your people. If you provide the direction that captures their imagination, the results will come."

The leaders set a visionary goal: Achieve 100 percent improvement in performance in three years. Later, when they presented this goal to their branch managers and other leaders, their people stood up and applauded.

> Trust your people. If you provide the direction that captures their spirit, you won't be able to stop them.

The leaders then joined employees to set intermediate goals together and to set in motion other functions of the Side by Side organizational leadership package. Three years later, the organization had improved "only" 90 percent. When this "failure" was presented at a leaders' conference, all applauded and congratulated one another — because 90 percent of a "wow" three-year goal was far better than the usual 8 to 12 percent "realistic" annual improvement most organizations shoot for.

Skill 19: Creating New Strategies

When you're aiming at visionary goals, simply doing the same work with more effort won't get you there.[5] It takes creative new strategies: new programs or projects that push

CREATIVE STRATEGIES TO GROW A LEMONADE BUSINESS	
GENERAL GROWTH STRATEGY	LEMONADE STAND EXAMPLES
SELL MORE OF EXISTING PRODUCTS & SERVICES TO CURRENT CUSTOMERS	• OPEN NEW STANDS ACROSS TOWN • STAY OPEN LONGER
ATTRACT NEW GROUPS OF CUSTOMERS TO EXISTING PRODUCTS	● SELL LEMONADE AT BUS STOPS DURING RUSH HOUR
SELL NEW PRODUCTS & SERVICES	• MAKE LEMONADE POPSICLES • MAKE HOT LEMON TEA TO SELL IN THE WINTER
IMPROVE & INNOVATE WITHIN THE PRODUCT OR SERVICE DELIVERY SYSTEM	• SELL BOTTLED LEMONADE TO SCHOOL & FACTORY CAFETERIAS • SELL LEMONADE STAND KITS & SUPPLIES AT TOY STORES
MOVE INTO NEW GEOGRAPHIC LOCATIONS (A DIFFICULT STRATEGY)	• RECRUIT A PARTNER TO OPEN LEMONADE STANDS IN ANOTHER CITY
ENTER NEW BUSINESS THROUGH VERTICAL INTEGRATION OR DIVERSIFICATION OF EXISTING SPECIALTIES	• BUY LEMON ORCHARDS OR A COMPANY THAT TRANSPORTS LEMONS • MAKE PEANUT BUTTER COOKIES TO SELL WITH LEMONADE.

the organization. Vastar invested in more advanced measuring skills and data analysis, and its geologists achieved greater success in finding productive drilling locations. This and other creative ideas helped Vastar exceed its visionary goals.

Most organizations' annual planning does not include visionary goals or creative strategies for achieving them. At best, there are annual budgets with small increases in spending and small growth projections. This is not so much planning as budgeting; it should be called "pludgeting."

Mehrdad Baghai, Stephen Coley, and David White, of the highly respected McKinsey and Company consulting firm, studied forty companies worldwide that had over 30 percent growth in shareholder return year after year. What did these high-growth companies — which included Coca-Cola–Amatil of Australia, Walt Disney, Gillette, Charles Schwab, and Home Depot — do that set them apart from run-of-the-mill companies? They concentrated on a few strategies at a time and developed them in a variety of ways. The same creative strategies (see table on page 188) can, when generalized, help your organization achieve its visionary goals.[6]

Organizational Goal Setting and Planning

Brainstorming possible new strategies is not enough; leaders and contributors must also select the best ones in which to invest time and money. Leaders using structured decision making are more successful at this than leaders who base decisions mostly on emotions and pressure from others. Greed and fear can blind managers to the facts; structured decision making helps leaders manage these negative emotions. The result is better strategies and higher productivity.[7]

The process takes time; fortunately, there is a way to tap into the creativity of people who are eager to help leaders make these decisions. The next one or two organizational levels below the top leaders can help achieve visionary goals and strategies through two-way goal setting and planning.

Like all other Side by Side skills, organizational planning is not a one-way, top-down process; it is two-way communication about goals and how to achieve them. All members of the organization must direct their daily activities toward the visionary goals. The leaders who have developed them must meet with team members and begin planning their work toward the goals.

True communication is, in practice, two-way. However, most organizational leaders disseminate their most important message — annual goals — by addressing a crowd in an auditorium, with employees sitting silently in long rows facing the podium for an hour or more. At the end, they ask for questions, and usually get only a few. The leaders grade their speeches by the number of questions or comments they get — the fewer, the better. How effective do you think such meetings are in motivating people?

Amoco Oil's Houston division conducted a six-month follow-up study of its goal-communication meetings.[8] It found that people attending the meetings

- could not remember the goals that were presented,

- did not think the company had goals, or

- could not even remember there had been a meeting.

Why didn't employees remember the meetings? Psychology research shows that people quickly forget information presented to them unless given the opportunity to work with it or discuss it.[9]

Participative management skills are key to successful organizational planning. Using structured brainstorming (chapter 9), Side by Side organizational leaders ask employees to think about overcoming barriers and achieving visionary goals. The purpose of the brainstorming is to come up with as many innovative ideas as possible for changing work processes and overcoming any problems that might arise as a result.

After planning meetings, leaders select the best ideas, based on their knowledge and other information. From the strategies that were proposed, team leaders and teams choose those most likely to achieve the goals. Even though not all the contributors' ideas on goals and strategies are used, productivity will still rise, because all members of the organization feel they have a voice in decisions. The shared decisions continue down through work processes, information systems, and even the processes used to make decisions and to reward and recognize accomplishments.

Contributors and leaders leave Side by Side planning meetings highly motivated, committed to the tough actions needed to achieve the visionary goals. Difficulties may arise if it becomes necessary to discontinue favorite products or services, as Andy Grove had to do at Intel. Another challenge is adding new products, services, or processes that require different knowledge and relationships. Vastar had to leave behind its popular and comfortable onshore wildcat drilling program to implement a new, riskier strategy of bidding for offshore oil leases in deep Gulf of Mexico waters. Fortunately, they were able to hire people with knowledge and experience in deepwater exploration and drilling.

Skill 20: Creating a Flexible Organization

Reacting quickly in a fast-changing business environment requires flexibility, especially in the structure of the organization. Developing a Side by Side organizational structure is a sure way of building an organization that responds to ideas and innovations proposed by all members of the team. The actions necessary include

- creating organizational charts;

- extending your boundaries and listening to others outside the organization;

- developing joint ventures, alliances, and partnerships side by side; and

- developing internal empowered, aligned, decentralized teams that move rapidly.

The reason this is the fifth organizational leadership skill instead of the first is that the leader cannot even think about the form or structure of the organization until the organizational goals and strategies are developed. The purpose of structure is to *implement* the strategies that are designed to achieve the goals.

Changing Charts

Often the first thing a newly promoted organizational leader decides to do is change the organizational chart. Change can make leaders feel out of control and make who reports to whom seem of overriding importance. To regain the feeling of control, they spend days, weeks, even months mulling over and redrawing organization charts, creating headaches for everyone involved. But the management chart is actually the least important aspect of the organization's structure. More crucial is putting the functions together to implement the necessary strategies.

There are, of course, times when restructuring is called for. A new organizational structure can be useful in responding to the development of new strategies, the introduction of new products or services, changes in customer needs, or the formation of a new alliance or partnership. In the volatile computer market of the 1990s, the leaders of Dell Computer Corporation modified their organizational structure three or four times a year to respond to customer changes. Their criterion was how best to capture and make money on each new opportunity.

Expanding Boundaries

To achieve visionary goals, organizational leaders must think of their organization as not just the employees inside but the customers, suppliers, allies, and partners outside as well. The organizational resources that must be structured are found both inside and outside.

Often managers and contributors treat customers, suppliers, and even essential business partners as second-class citizens. It's not an uncommon mistake to withhold important information from such "outsiders," who can contribute vital information for decisions involving services and product development. The Ford Taurus, one of the most successful new automobiles built during the 1980s, was created through teamwork between Ford engineers, factory workers, customers, and key parts suppliers. Ford leaders treated the "outsiders" as equals with Ford employees, encouraging open communication and a flow of creative ideas. Ford engineers listened to customers' feature preferences. The result was one of Ford's all-time best-selling automobiles.

Success Factors for Joint Ventures

Factor	Competitive Approach	Side by Side Approach
Primary Discussion & Planning Focus	How much money will my company make?	What new actions will we take together that will create new wealth?
Objectives	Financial only; project-focused	Financial, operational, cultural (working together); both project-focused and others
Planning	Financial planning only	Financial, operational, cultural planning
Support for front-line workers who must implement	None, not even communicating objectives	Involve them in partnership workshops that provide coordination & implementation mechanisms
Employees' Perception of Management	We have to guess what management wants & figure out for ourselves how to reach it	Management wants us to be two-way & supportive & to contribute ideas to the goals & strategies
Short-Term Results	Joint venture fails, consumes resources	Joint venture succeeds, provides return on investments
Long-Term Results	Goes to court; partners never work together again	Smoothly & rapidly come together to capitalize on new opportunities

Developing Joint Ventures

Most joint ventures, alliances, and partnerships fail. What characterizes the ones that succeed? There is a certain mind-set, characteristic of Side by Side leaders, that correlates well with successful joint ventures. As with other Side by Side Leadership principles, this approach has to do with open communication and mutual respect.

Led with Side by Side principles, joint ventures, alliances, and partnerships can be successful. Success comes from working together from the very beginning.

Empowering Teams

In the late 1980s, General Electric, under Jack Welch's leadership, gave decentralized business units the authority to make decisions and move quickly. In most organizations, the biggest delay in implementing new products and services is waiting for a decision by someone higher in the organization. Some otherwise knowledgeable organizational leaders, including founders, fall into the trap of thinking they have all the answers and micromanaging everyone's work.

Side by Side organizational leaders know they don't have to tell people what to do, day after day. With all leaders and contributors signed on to the organizational values, visionary goals, and strategies, they know they can shift power to their functional teams and rely on their motivated employees' creative energy to keep the company responsive and competitive.

The Leadership Revolution

The assembly line was the first true innovation in American manufacturing. Since that early twentieth century revolution, innovations by other thinkers, managers, and industrial engineers, such as Frederick Taylor and other

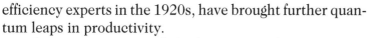

efficiency experts in the 1920s, have brought further quantum leaps in productivity.

The quantum wave of the late twentieth century was empowerment and shared management teams. This shift in management philosophy contributed to eighteen straight years of almost unbroken growth in productivity. But the value of contributors' insight, intelligence, knowledge, creativity, and experience did not become immediately and simultaneously apparent to all leaders.

By the 1980s, most leaders recognized the importance of getting innovations into effect rapidly and competitively. At one Asea Brown Boveri (ABB) electronics plant in the American South, the production cycle time on one of its major products was twelve days. This was deemed too long, so engineers devised new work processes, and managers directed assemblers and testers to start using them. No questions, no comments, just do it.

After one month, assembly time was down to nine days. The managers and engineers gave themselves a pat on the back. There was only one problem. After three months, assembly time had regressed to twelve days.

> There's nothing like a motivated work force to boost productivity.

At this point, the leaders decided to train the assemblers and testers to be a shared-management team and to take responsibility for improving their own work processes. Members of the team took turns planning and leading the weekly team meeting.

Within six months the team had reduced their production time to three days. Not only did it stay at that level, but the team worked with purchasing and parts inventory groups over the next year to reduce the total time to two days. Using their own ideas and making their own decisions, the team increased their productivity sixfold.

Leaders have always sought creative suggestions for improving organizational performance. Here's the beauty of shared-management teams: not only is the knowledge and creativity of all contributors made available, but all

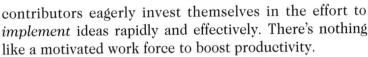

contributors eagerly invest themselves in the effort to *implement* ideas rapidly and effectively. There's nothing like a motivated work force to boost productivity.

The five Side by Side organizational leadership skills, working synergistically, help the organization respond quickly to external and internal environmental changes. They are key to sustaining the vitality and longevity of the company.

Take a look at your organization today. Does it need these leadership skills? If so, you may be the one who leads it to success.

Part

IV

Applying the Formula for Success

Side by Side Leadership is a system model for human performance improvement. Its formula may seem complicated and it may appear to have many elements to keep track of, but when you begin to put it into practice you'll see that Side by Side is a natural way of leading that becomes easier the more you use it. Your leadership skills and instincts will improve, your contributors will become more knowledgeable and motivated, and together you will achieve outstanding results for your organization.

Side by Side Leadership is built from the following components:

The Seven Principles:

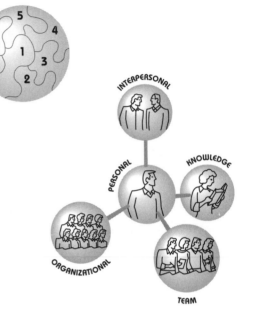

1. Two-Way Street
2. Interaction Fields
3. Visionary Goals
4. Focused Creativity
5. Structured Participation
6. Proven Knowledge
7. Transferred Authority

The Five Spheres of Influence:

1. Personal
2. Knowledge
3. Interpersonal
4. Team
5. Organizational

The Twenty Skills:

1. Achieving Personal Visionary Goals
2. Practicing Honesty and Fairness
3. Maintaining Objectivity

4. Acquiring Knowledge
5. Sharing Knowledge
6. Transforming Knowledge

7. Two-Way Listening
8. Mutual Contributing
9. Connecting Visionary Goals
10. Diverse Networking

11. Managing the Interface
12. Setting Team Goals
13. Using Structured Team Skills
14. Coordinating Team Roles
15. Increasing Team Capacity

16. Identifying Opportunities and Threats
17. Living Organizational Values
18. Setting Organizational Visionary Goals
19. Creating New Strategies
20. Creating a Flexible Organization

In addition to the tips I've provided for each ingredient, the examples and case studies are models you can emulate. You can also develop your own leadership improvement exercises. In this section, I will offer you sample exercises to help you practice each of the seven principles. I will also provide you with an assessment questionnaire that will help you determine your strengths in the five leadership spheres of influence. Finally, I will offer you my views on where a world full of Side by Side leaders could take us.

Chapter 17

Becoming a Side by Side Leader

Practical Applications of the Seven Principles of
Side by Side Leadership

The basic concept of leading side by side can be practiced a number of ways. The next time you need to plan a project that includes a group of people, consider gathering them together to brainstorm ideas for how to do the project. Whenever you need to work with another person, sit down at a table and plan together. Be sure to get out from behind the desk. Work side by side instead of using a desk to communicate dominance.

I worked for an executive who invited his managers to ride with him in his car to meetings both close by and out of town. He used those trips to share his vision and ideas for the future of our organization, and to ask our opinions of his ideas. As we sat in the front seat of his car, we were definitely talking and listening to each other side by side. Sometimes on these outings he asked me how things were going in my area of responsibility. The car trips were special because he made me feel I was important.

The Side by Side Leadership model can be applied to problems that occur on the fly. A manager in a high-tech company wanted to recognize an engineer in his organization for outstanding performance. The manager's problem was that he did not know how or whether to involve the engineer's team leader in presenting the award and bonus. The manager heard about Side by Side and immediately got the idea to go to the team leader and plan the recognition together. A potential conflict was avoided, and the manager and team leader recognized the engineer together with a united front.

The best way to improve your Side by Side Leadership performance is to identify and practice new skills. Continual practice will embed these skills into your natural behavior patterns. Below are my ideas for practicing the seven principles. Challenge yourself to come up with your own skills and action steps.

Principle 1: Two-Way Street

Side by Side Leadership requires two-way interactions at all levels. One of the best exercises to learn this skill is to ask contributors to share their ideas about problems and decisions before you present your own. As they speak, listen to their ideas. One good way to indicate, without words, that you think the contributor's ideas are important is to visibly write the ideas down. To become good at leading two-way, practice once a day by asking people their ideas on an issue, waiting until they are finished before presenting your own.

Principle 2: Interaction Fields

Leaders can improve performance by adding new resources or using existing resources more creatively. They do this by using people and other resources from interaction fields outside their own work group. If you are a team leader or manager, draw on paper the other teams' and departments' interaction fields that are close to yours in terms of purpose and work processes. Identify how you can incorporate resources from those groups to help your team achieve its visionary goals.

If you are an organizational leader, take a few minutes to draw the interaction field map for the major external influences on your organization. Consider customers, suppliers, competitors, investors, your industry, the economy, government, society, and changes in the physical environment. Brainstorm how new types of relationships with those influences could improve your organization's success.

Principle 3: Visionary Goals

Develop a visionary goal for your life. Practice sharing your personal visionary goals with a few of your friends or family members. If you have a good visionary goal, the first time a friend hears it, she will say "Wow!" The "Wow!" response ensures that your goal is reach-out enough to pull breakthrough ideas. Follow up by asking your friend what creative ideas she can think of to achieve your visionary goal.

You've learned that it's not enough to develop visionary goals; you need to develop and implement creative strategies to achieve the goals. A. L. Williams, a public school coach with a large family, set a goal to save $1 million within five years so that he could provide a college education for his children. (Notice that he wanted wealth not for its own sake, but to do something for others.) Williams knew that he needed to use creative strategies to achieve the goal. He left the field of coaching and started a life insurance company that sold term life insurance at a lower price than the major companies. Williams became a multimillionaire and helped many other people along the way.

Visionary goals succeed with teams and organizations, too. Team and organization visionary goals should be shared to stimulate people to use new and creative work methods and business strategies.

Principle 4: Focused Creativity

There are a number of actions you can take to improve your creativity and that of other people. Begin by doubling the number of possible solutions you come up with for problems. Most people can think of only one or two solutions for a problem. Train yourself to come up with at least six solutions every time. If the problem is significant, develop at least twenty solutions. Side by Side comes into its own when a small group can come up with twenty solutions for a problem in twenty minutes. In the beginning, when you work alone, brainstorming twenty different solutions for a significant problem may take a week or two. With practice, you'll come up with twenty solutions in one hour. It takes practice to suppress negative self-talk about wild ideas, to think outside the box, and to find the grains of truth where the wild ideas hide.

Principle 5: Structured Participation

Here's the main planning tip for getting 100 percent participation in meetings: Before the meeting, prepare written instructions for engaging everyone. To develop these instructions, first write down the work you want to accomplish in the meeting. For example, you might want to identify and select the major causes of a current critical problem, or improve the quality of work that a group you lead performs. Write down the instructions you will give the group. Imagine that you wish to improve the quality of work that your group performs. In this meeting, you want your team to identify the work group's main customers and the level of quality they want in your services and products. The specific instructions you would read to your team might be the following:

1. "Write down on your paper the names of our major customers." Allow four to five minutes for your contributors to write down their ideas.

2. Say to each person on your team, "Read from your list one of the customers you wrote down." Get one idea per person, and continue until all ideas are collected. As you go around the group, be sure you include one of your own ideas after you have listed one idea for each of your team members.

3. As they read, list the customers on flip-chart paper where team members can see them.

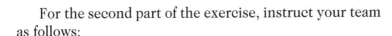

For the second part of the exercise, instruct your team as follows:

1. "Write down the quality our customers want in our products and services." Once again, allow four to five minutes for the team members to write down their ideas.

2. Going around the group, get one idea per person on customer quality requirements. Repeat this process until all of the ideas are gathered. When you are finished, the team will have produced a long list of potential quality areas to improve.

3. Now ask the team members to discuss which of the quality areas seem to be causing the most trouble. After a few minutes, ask the team to vote on the three most important quality areas to improve.

The above planned participation activities promote every team member's participation in the important area of improving quality. Because every single team member is asked for his ideas, all team members will walk out of the meeting committed to improving quality in the three areas that were selected.

Principle 6: Proven Knowledge

Many small decisions and problems are discussed over the course of a day in meetings and conversations. More often than not, people have less knowledge than emotional opinions about the decision or problem under discussion. In meetings or conversations, when solutions or alternative decisions are being discussed, ask, "What knowledge do we have that we can use to help solve this problem or make this decision?" Try to identify for yourself places both inside and outside your organization where valid knowledge exists that can be used to solve the most frequently discussed problems.

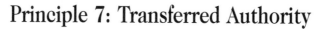

Principle 7: Transferred Authority

A great way for a leader to begin sharing more decision-making power is to identify all the decisions the leader currently makes. You can try this on yourself. List all decisions that you make, approve, or review that are related to the work you do alone and with other people.

To get a more complete picture, gather the people who work with you and ask them to list the decisions you make, approve, or review. With their input, the list may be much longer. Ask the group to identify one decision they think they could make without your approval or review. When they do so, ask them what additional knowledge or skills they need to make the decision on their own. Develop and implement a plan to transfer the decision and the knowledge to the group or team.

I will be putting other skills and action steps on the Internet. If you develop a skill or practice activity that works, please share it with me and others at sidebyside.com.

Chapter 18

Where Are You Now?

Your Individual Formula for Leadership Improvement

A major tenet of Side by Side Leadership is that there is no one leadership pattern of success. Chapter 4 presented the five spheres of leadership influence that leaders can use within the various interaction fields inside and outside the organization. Within each of the spheres of influence, there are five levels of competency: none, low, medium, high, and very high. The "very high" level is the standard set by world-class leaders — Gandhi in personal leadership, Thomas Edison in knowledge leadership, Jack Welch of GE in organizational leadership.

An individual leader — you, for example — could be rated anywhere from level 1 to level 5 for any of the five spheres. The variety of leadership patterns includes all the combinations of competency levels — 3,125 different combinations, if you ignore the finer gradations. One leader is successful with a level 4 in all five spheres. Another leader has a level 5 in one sphere and level 3's in the other four and is equally successful.

I invite you to do an initial self-assessment of your current pattern for leadership success. The following exercise will help you determine which sphere is currently your strongest. Your score will also indicate which might be your weaker spheres. Remember, it's not necessary or even realistic to be high in all five spheres. Most leaders can be highly proficient in only one or two spheres of influence at a time.

Your Self-Assessment

In each of the four sections of the self-assessment, place a check mark next to the statements that are most true about you at this time in your career. You can mark more than one check for each question.

A. Of the following, which do you enjoy?

_____1. Work tasks that line up with your personal purpose, goals, or interests.

_____2. Acquiring and sharing knowledge.

_____3. Interpersonal tasks (one-on-one interactions, networking, working with one to four other individuals).

_____4. Working in groups, making sure work is coordinated, leading teams, facilitating meetings, and other team tasks.

_____5. Reading, thinking, and working on strategic direction and how the organization as a whole can perform better.

B. What kind of advice do people inside and outside your organization most often ask of you?

_____1. Personal problems related to career goals, life purpose, and meaning in life.

_____2. Problems and questions related to one or more of your areas of technical or knowledge expertise.

_____3. How to get along with others, motivate others, or solve and mediate interpersonal conflicts.

_____4. How to plan meetings, set team goals, and work with groups or teams.

_____5. Suggestions for how to fix organizational problems or problems related to being more successful with customers, suppliers, and others outside the organization.

C. In which of the following areas have you had the most training and personal study during the past three to four years?

_____1. Personal effectiveness, ethics, personal goal setting, time management, 7 *Habits of Highly Effective People* training.

_____2. Courses and training related to technical, scientific, or special knowledge in performing tasks (examples: sales training, engineering tools, science or business classes).

_____3. Conferences or training that you attended, primarily to meet and network with other people, that involved listening and interpersonal skills training and individual coaching.

_____4. Courses or training on teamwork, team skills, team leadership, and team or small group coaching.

_____5. Training, courses, and reading books on organizational leadership, business and industry trends, strategy formation, innovative human resource practices, and organizational development.

D. When I am anxious or under stress for personal or professional reasons, the stress

_____1. does not interfere with achieving my visionary goals and daily disciplines.

_____2. does not interfere with my reading, research on the Internet, classes, or my search for new knowledge.

_____3. does not spill over into conflicts with friends, colleagues, bosses, co-workers, or family.

_____4. does not cause me to argue or say things in meetings I later regret.

_____5. does not interfere with my ability to think creatively about organizational strategies and resources inside and outside the organization, or to lead organizational improvements.

E. Recent successes?

_____1. Personal: I have had recent measurable success on at least three of my strategies or plans related to achieving my personal visionary goals in the last three months.

_____2. Knowledge: I have used my technical or scientific knowledge and skills to achieve a major success for my organization within the last three months.

_____3. Interpersonal: I am a good listener and have at least ten friends and acquaintances who have helped me informally in the last three months.

_____4. Team: I am a leader or key contributor on a team that achieved a 25 percent improvement or greater result in the last three months.

_____5. Organizational: I have had a major influence in my organization, making major strategic or organizational improvements that have resulted in at least 20 percent or greater improvement in organizational results.

Scoring Instructions

For all sections, count the number of checks on the spaces next to number 1. These are your Personal Leadership responses. Put the total on the line below next to "Personal Leadership." Count the number of checks on the spaces next to number 2. These are your Knowledge Leadership responses. Put the total in the box below next to "Knowledge Leadership." Continue with number 3, Interpersonal Leadership; number 4, Team Leadership; and number 5, Organizational Leadership.

_____ Personal Leadership

_____ Knowledge Leadership

_____ Interpersonal Leadership

_____ Team Leadership

_____ Organizational Leadership

The larger the number, the stronger you are in that leadership sphere of influence. After you have identified your top one or two current leadership strengths, you can draw your leadership pattern. Put today's date at the top of your current pattern. In the space below, draw your self-assessment leadership pattern. Use the size of circle that corresponds to your leadership assessment. (See my example on the next page).

$$\textcircled{1} \quad \textcircled{2} \quad \bigcirc 3 \quad \bigcirc 4 \quad \bigcirc 5$$

Draw your leadership pattern here:

Knowledge   +   +   Interpersonal

              +   Personal

Organizational   +   +   Team

Below is an example of my leadership pattern today, as I am reviewing the last few chapters of *Side by Side Leadership*. Notice that my strongest leadership sphere is knowledge, which fits with what I needed to synthesize research and organizational case studies for this book and my clients.

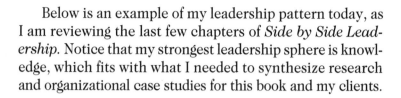

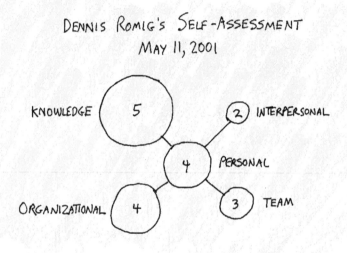

DENNIS ROMIG'S SELF-ASSESSMENT
MAY 11, 2001

KNOWLEDGE 5
INTERPERSONAL 2
PERSONAL 4
ORGANIZATIONAL 4
TEAM 3

Remember that it is neither possible nor necessary to be highly competent in all five spheres at one time. Notice in my pattern that the team sphere is not that big currently, even though I have won awards on my teamwork consulting and writing. I have not had time to keep that dynamic as strong as I'd like with all of the leadership and organizational consulting that I do. Your leadership pattern should adjust to the situation or tasks you are currently involved with.

Look at the pattern you drew on page 209. How does it match your current job and interests? One leader in one of my workshops discovered that his job required him to be a knowledge leader in a technical area, but his competency and interests were more in interpersonal leadership. He made a career change and got a job where he could better use his interpersonal leadership skills.

Consider the sphere in which you're strongest. How could you better use that sphere to succeed in your current job? If you're strong in knowledge leadership, perhaps you could do presentations, conduct training, or write articles where you could help your organization and other individuals.

Is there a sphere that you are low in that is detracting from your overall performance? You can build your own formula for improvement by deciding which one or two of the leadership spheres to focus on. If you work with teams or groups, you can enhance your team leadership skills to reap quick dividends.

The five-sphere assessment is subjective, and most people overestimate their competence. If you want a more objective evaluation, go back to the skills under each sphere of influence and measure your ability in each skill and the frequency with which you use it.

Review and practice the skills presented in this book for the sphere you want to improve. According to Jay Conger, director of the University of Southern California's Leadership Institute, and studies by the National Research Council, skill training and practice are the most proven methods for improving performance, although continuous practice must be sustained over a number of years.[1]

Improving in one sphere of leadership influence can produce spillover improvements in the other four spheres. For example, an increase in team productivity affects overall organizational success. Well-run, participative team meetings spill over to better interpersonal relationships between team members.

Many men and women work primarily to bring home money for their families. It's not enough to have children; they want to provide a good life for them as well. In one leadership training session I facilitated, I asked the participants to choose which of their personal career values overlapped with their current job. Most of the men and women had only one value: to work in order to bring home a paycheck and support their family.

Side by Side vs. Top-Down Leadership

Side by Side	Top-Down
Skill 1: Achieving personal visionary goals	Striving for personal power & wealth
Skill 2: Practicing honesty & fairness	Succeeding at any cost & losing trust
Skill 3: Maintaining objectivity	It's okay to lose one's temper
Skill 4: Acquiring knowledge	Using only what you learned in the past
Skill 5: Sharing knowledge	Hoarding knowledge
Skill 6: Transforming knowledge	Not leveraging knowledge
Skill 7: Two-way listening	Leading by commanding & talking
Skill 8: Mutual contributing	Always maintaining superior status
Skill 9: Connecting visionary goals	Promoting one's own goals
Skill 10: Diverse networking	Interacting with only a few people who are similar to oneself
Skill 11: Managing the interface	Thinking only about one's own department
Skill 12: Setting team goals	Focusing on one's own priorities
Skill 13: Using structured team skills	Not providing team training
Skill 14: Coordinating team roles	Dictating what work each person must do
Skill 15: Increasing team capacity	Having people do the same work day after day
Skill 16: Identifying opportunities and threats	Worrying only about problems inside the organization
Skill 17: Living organizational values	Letting financial success override all else
Skill 18: Setting organizational visionary goals	No real vision; no organizational goals
Skill 19: Creating new strategies	Continuing to use the same products & services
Skill 20: Creating a flexible organization	Believing all innovations & decisions should come from the top

Up to this point, the leadership training had been rolling along at a nice pace, but the sudden realization of how empty and valueless their work was stunned those participants. Their faces reflected their confusion, frustration, and feelings of being lost. They had not developed personal work goals based on their values, life purpose, or interests. Their personal leadership was low.

Parents shortchange their children if they hate the jobs that bring in the money. They are not teaching by example a most important lesson: find or create a career that fulfills you. The children may grow up with their material needs met, but lost emotionally because they have no fulfilling purpose themselves. A good job cannot just bring in money; it must also provide fulfillment.

Side by Side Leadership guides leaders in their quest to achieve personal fulfillment. The Side by Side leaders described in this book felt they were living their lives on the edge every day. Excitement tinged their voices, and energy emanated from the bounce in their steps. Their lives at work and at home were like an adventure with great friends. They had forward momentum toward their highest personal goals. Stress, conflicts, and setbacks did not have the usual disruptive force in their lives.

The contributors who worked around these Side by Side leaders also felt excited and energized about work and their lives as a whole. Their leaders encouraged them to find and achieve personal meaning and value in their lives.

Making a Better World

Side by Side Leadership can nurture and grow a world full of leaders like Gandhi, Martin Luther King Jr., and Cesar Chavez, who lived to improve the moral and ethical climate for all. We can create more Thomas Edisons, Einsteins, and Jane Goodalls, whose passion for their ideas and knowledge transforms us. It is possible to develop new Alfred P. Sloans and Jack Welches to lead enduring organizations that provide meaningful jobs.

Side by Side leaders will create wealth and solutions to the world's problems that cannot now be imagined. They will create peaceful solutions to world conflicts, in which all parties and their succeeding generations experience wealth instead of decades of desolation. They will solve problems of the environment.

Side by Side leaders of the future will be able to use natural systems thinking and their whole brains in ways adults of today cannot imagine. Leaders who lead to create abundance plus fulfillment integrate their emotions and thinking. This is in contrast with most human tragedies and wars, which are due to unchecked emotions or cold, unfeeling thinking. Emotion and rationality will be integrated side by side in the leaders of the future.

The time has come to perfect a new model of leadership. Side by Side Leadership is a scientific and natural systems–based model. This book has presented the latest research and my thinking on improving personal, knowledge, interpersonal, team, and organizational productivity by applying natural systems thinking.

In the next few years, more research will be conducted and presented in other publications and on the Internet. As you apply the principles and skills of Side by Side Leadership and make new discoveries for yourself, I would appreciate your sharing them with me at my web site, www.sidebyside.com. I look forward to working and learning side by side with you to create an abundant and peaceful world.

> Side by Side leaders will create wealth and solutions to the world's problems that cannot now be imagined.

Notes

Chapter 1

1   Hogan, Robert, Gordon J. Curphy, and Joyce Hogan (1994), "What we know about leadership effectiveness and personality." *American Psychologist* 49(6) (June 1994), 493–504.

The reciprocal and co-dependent behaviors in organizations using top-down leadership resulted in a closed organizational system. It has also been documented that top-down subordinates in asymmetrical relationships steal, sabotage, lie, and distort upward communication. McMillan, Jill J., and Nickol A. Northern (1995), "Organizational codependency: The creation and maintenance of closed systems." *Management Communication Quarterly* 9(1) (Aug. 1995), 6–45.

2   Agnes, Michael (ed.), and Andrew Sparks (1998), *Webster's New World Dictionary of American English*. Springfield, Mass.: Merriam-Webster.

3   Locke, Edwin A. (1991), *The Essence of Leadership: The Four Keys to Leading Successfully*. Lexington, Mass.: Lexington-Macmillan, 2.

4   Bass, Bernard M., and Ralph M. Stogdill (1981), *Bass and Stogdill's Handbook of Leadership: Theory, Research, and Managerial Applications*. New York: Free Press.

5   Greenleaf, Robert K. (1983), *Servant Leadership: A Journey into the Nature of Legitimate Power and Greatness*. Mahwah, N.J.: Paulist Press.

6   Goleman, Daniel (1994), *Emotional Intelligence: Why It Can Matter More Than I.Q.* New York: Bantam Books, 161–162.

Kelly, Robert E. (1998), *How to Be a Star at Work: Nine Breakthrough Strategies You Need to Succeed*. New York: Time Business.

Chapter 2

1   Romig, Dennis (2001), *The Science of Side by Side*. Austin: Performance Research Press.

2   Graen, George, Michael A. Novak, and Patricia Sommerkamp (1982), "The effects of leader-member exchange and job

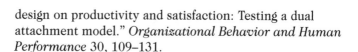

design on productivity and satisfaction: Testing a dual attachment model." *Organizational Behavior and Human Performance* 30, 109–131.

3   Scandura, Terri A., and George B. Graen (1984), "Moderating effects of initial leader-member exchange status on the effects of a leadership intervention." *Journal of Applied Psychology* 69(3), 428–436.

4   Romig, Dennis (1996), *Breakthrough Teamwork: Outstanding Results Using Structured Teamwork.* Austin: Performance Research Press.

5   Bragg, J. E., and I. E. Andrews (1973), "Participative decision making: An experimental study in a hospital." *Journal of Applied Behavioral Science* 9(6), 727–735.

6   Mayo, G. Elton (1933), *The Human Problems of an Industrial Civilization.* New York: Macmillan.

Drucker, Peter (1973), *Management: Tasks, Responsibilities, Practices.* New York: Harper & Row.

Lewin, Kurt (1951), *Field Theory in Social Science: Selected Theoretical Papers.* Cartwright, D. (ed.). New York: Harper & Row.

McGregor, D. (1960), *The Human Side of Enterprise.* New York: McGraw-Hill.

Blake, Robert, and Jane Mouton (1964), *The Managerial Grid.* Houston: Gulf.

Trist, E. L., G. W. Higgin, H. Murray, and A. B. Pollock (1963), *Organizational Choice.* London: Tavistock Publications.

7   Peters, Thomas J., and Robert H. Waterman Jr. (1982), *In Search of Excellence: Lessons from American's Best-Run Companies.* New York: Harper & Row.

Bass, Bernard M. (1985), *Leadership and Performance Beyond Expectations.* New York: Free Press.

Covey, Stephen R. (1989), *The 7 Habits of Highly Effective People: Restoring the Character Ethic.* New York: Simon & Schuster.

Senge, Peter M. (1990), *The Fifth Discipline: The Art and Practice of the Learning Organization.* New York: Doubleday Currency.

Wheatley, Margaret J. (1992), *Leadership and the New Science*. San Francisco: Berrett-Koehler.

Papero, Daniel V. (1990), *Bowen Family Systems Theory*. Needham Heights, Mass.: Allyn & Bacon.

Kerr, Michael, and Murray Bowen (1988), *Family Evaluation: An Approach Based upon Bowen Theory*. New York: W. W. Norton.

Comella, Patricia A., Joyce Bader, Judith Ball, Kathleen Wiseman, and Ruth Sagar (1996), *The Emotional Side of Organizations: Applications of Bowen Theory*. Washington, D.C.: Georgetown Family Center.

Chapter 3

1 Fiorina, Carly (2000), "Strategy and execution for the digital renaissance." Speech delivered Sept. 27, 2000 to Chief Executives' Club of Boston.

Chapter 4

1 Key elements of Bass's transformational leadership model that overlapped the personal, interpersonal, knowledge, and organizational spheres of Side by Side Leadership contributed to improved performance. Bass, Bernard (1997), "Does the transactional-transformation leadership paradigm transcend organizational and national boundaries?" *American Psychologist* 52(2), 130–139.

Additional support for five spheres of leadership comes from Collins, who in researching how good companies become great discovered that the successful executive leaders combined high personal leadership (strong determination and humility), knowledge leadership (choosing a few things for their companies to excel in), and interpersonal leadership (knowing how to choose and relate to good people), and that they led the organization through values and vision. Collins, Jim (2001), "Level 5 leadership: The triumph of humility and fierce resolve." *Harvard Business Review* 79(1) (Jan. 2001), 67–76.

2 Technical and industry knowledge were the two most important criteria in leadership evaluation by successful

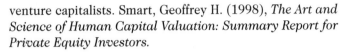

venture capitalists. Smart, Geoffrey H. (1998), *The Art and Science of Human Capital Valuation: Summary Report for Private Equity Investors.*

3   Bass and Stogdill (1990).

4   Lam, Simon S. K., and John Schaubroeck (2000), "A field experiment testing frontline opinion leaders as change agents." *Journal of Applied Psychology* 85(6), 987–995.

Chapter 5

1   Romig, Dennis (2001), *The Science of Side by Side.* Austin: Performance Research Press.

2   Wagner, John A. III, Carrie R. Leana, Edwin A. Locke, and David W. Schweiger (1997), "Cognitive and motivational frameworks in U.S. research on participation: A meta-analysis of primary effects." *Journal of Organizational Behavior* 18, 49–65.

Romig (1996).

3   Tarlov, Alvin, and Robert F. St. Peter, eds. (2000), *The Society and Population Health Reader, Vol. 2: A State Perspective.* New York: New Press.

Chapter 6

1   Paying attention to and connecting to the external environment's threats and opportunities was a distinction between surviving companies and bankrupt companies. D'Aveni, Richard A., and Ian C. MacMillan (1990), "Crisis and the content of managerial communications: A study of the focus of attention of top managers in surviving and failing firms." *Administrative Science Quarterly* 35, 634–657.

2   Barnard, Chester (1938), *The Functions of the Executive.* Cambridge, Mass.: Harvard University Press.

3   Lowe, Janet C. (1998), *Jack Welch Speaks: Wisdom from the World's Greatest Business Leader.* New York: John Wiley & Sons, 75.

4   Barker, Joel (1993), *Paradigm Pioneers.* Burnsville, Minn.: ChartHouse International.

Chapter 7

1 Katzenbach, Jon R., and Douglas K. Smith (1993), *The Wisdom of Teams: Creating the High-Performance Organization.* Boston: Harvard Business School Press.

2 Locke, Edwin, and Gary Latham (1984), *Goal Setting: A Motivational Technique That Works!* Englewood Cliffs, N.J.: Prentice-Hall.

3 Locke and Latham (1984), 460.

4 Ivancevich, J. M., and J. T. McMahon (1982), "The effects of goal setting, external feedback, and self-generated feedback on outcome variables: A field experiment." *Academy of Management Journal* 25, 359–372.

5 Lawrence, L. C., and P. C. Smith (1955), "Group decision and employee participation." *Journal of Applied Psychology* 39(5), 334–337.

6 This claim is based on the following studies:

Buller, P. F. (1988), "Long-term performance effects of goal setting and team building interventions in an underground silver mine." *Organization Development Journal* (Summer 1988), 82–87.

Petty, M. M., B. Singleton, and D. W. Connell (1992), "An experimental evaluation of an organizational incentive plan in the electric utility industry." *Journal of Applied Psychology* 77(4), 427–436.

Pritchard, R. D., S. D. Jones, P. L. Roth, K. K. Stuebing, and S. E. Ekeberg (1988), "Effects of group feedback, goal setting, and incentives on organizational productivity." *Journal of Applied Psychology* 73(2), 337–358.

Reimer, R. A. (1992), "The effects of productivity, gain sharing, and employee involvement in the innovation process on job performance and organizational commitment." *Dissertation Abstracts International* 53(2), 1096B.

7 Ludwig, Timothy, and E. S. Geller (1997), "Assigned versus participatory goal setting and response generalization: Managing injury control among professional pizza deliverers." *Journal of Applied Psychology* 82, 253–261.

8 Buller, P. F., and C. H. Bell Jr. (1986), "Effects of team building and goal setting on productivity: A field experiment." *Academy of Management Journal* 29(2), 305–328.

Reimer, R. A. (1992).

Chapter 8

1 Csikszentmihalyi, Mihaly (1996), *Creativity: Flow and the Psychology of Discovery and Invention.* New York: Harper Perennial, 98

2 Romig (1996).

3 Kolb, Judith (1990), "Relationships between leader behaviors and team performance in research and nonresearch teams." (Doctoral dissertation.) Denver: University of Denver.

4 Barker, Joel (1985), *Discovering the Future: The Business of Paradigms.* St. Paul, Minn.: ILI Press.

Chapter 9

1 Gryskiewicz, Stanley S. (1988) "Trial by fire in an industrial setting: A practical evaluation of three creative problem solving techniques," in Kaufman, G., and K. Gronhaug (eds.), *Innovations: A Cross-Disciplinary Perspective.* Oslo: Norwegian University Press, 205–232.

2 Diehl, M., and W. Stroebe (1987), "Productivity loss in brainstorming groups: Toward the solution of a riddle." *Journal of Personality and Social Psychology* 53(3), 497–509.

Gist, M. (1989), "The influence of training method on self-efficacy and idea generation among managers." *Personnel Psychology* 42, 787–805.

3 Dunnette, M. D., J. Campbell, and K. Jaastad (1963), "The effect of group participation on brainstorming effectiveness for two industrial samples." *Journal of Applied Psychology* 47(1), 30–37.

Delbecq, A. L., A. H. Van de Ven, and D. H. Gustafson (1975), *Group Techniques for Program Planning: A Guide to Nominal Group and Delphi Processes.* Glenview, Ill: Scott, Foresman.

Diehl and Stroebe (1987), 497.

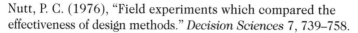

Nutt, P. C. (1976), "Field experiments which compared the effectiveness of design methods." *Decision Sciences* 7, 739–758.

4   Gryskiewicz (1988).

5   Diehl and Stroebe (1987).

6   Narramore, K. D. (1992), "The use of focus groups for organizational research: The effects of moderated focus groups versus self-moderated focus groups on employee self-disclosure and idea generation." *Dissertation Abstracts International* 53(7), 3822B.

7   Goldstein, Arnold, and Melvin Sorcher (1974), *Changing Supervisor Behavior.* New York: Elsevier Science, 70–82.

Chapter 10

1   Csikszentmihalyi (1996).

2   Csikszentmihalyi (1996), 49–50.

3   Wood, Robert E., Anthony J. Mento, and Edwin A. Locke (1987), "Task complexity as a moderator of goal effects: A meta-analysis." *Journal of Applied Psychology* 72(3), 416–425.

4   Leonard, Dorothy (1995), *Wellsprings of Knowledge: Building and Sustaining the Sources of Innovation.* Boston: Harper Business School Press, 15.

5   Leonard (1995), 15.

6   Rogers, Everett (1995), *Diffusion of Innovations* (4th ed.). New York: Free Press.

Chapter 11

1   Gist (1989).

2   Diehl and Stroebe (1987).

3   Seligman, Martin E. P. (1990), *Learned Optimism.* New York: Pocket Books.

4   Bandura, A. (1997), *Self-Efficacy: The Exercise of Control.* New York: W. H. Freeman.

5   Plunkett, D. J. (1990), "The creative organization: An empirical investigation of the importance of participation in decision-making." *Journal of Creative Behavior* 24(2), 140–148.

Chapter 12

1 Csikszentmihalyi (1990), 107.

2 Csikszentmihalyi (1990), 4.

3 Covey Leadership Center (1996), *Synergy: Creating Unstoppable People, Teams, and Organizations.* Ogden, Utah: Covey Leadership Center.

4 Lowe (1998), 35.

5 Harrison, Lawrence (1992), *Who Prospers? How Cultural Values Shape Economic and Political Success.* New York: Basic Books.

6 Fukuyama, Francis (1995), *Trust: The Social Virtues and the Creation of Prosperity.* New York: Free Press.

7 Doering, Rena Ruth Rebecca (1998), "Ethical decision-making in a business setting: Perceptions of employees." (Doctoral dissertation, Texas A&M University, College Station, Texas.)

8 Beecroft, John (1956), *Kipling: A Selection of His Stories and Poems.* New York: Doubleday.

9 Hazucha, J. F. (1991), "Success, jeopardy and performance: contrasting managerial outcomes and their predictors." (Unpublished doctoral dissertation, University of Minnesota, Minneapolis.)

10 Ruzicka, Mary F. (1988), "A psychological study examining how differentiation of self and stress relate to adult's scientific and engineering creativity." (Unpublished doctoral dissertation, Seton Hall University, South Orange, N.J.)

11 Goleman, Daniel (1995), *Emotional Intelligence.* New York: Bantam Books, 171.

12 Allman, John (2000), *Evolving Brains.* New York: W. H. Freeman.

13 Yukl, Gary A. (1994), *Leadership in Organizations* (3rd ed.). Englewood Cliffs, N.J.: Prentice-Hall.

14 Grove, Andrew S. (1996), *Only the Paranoid Survive: How to Exploit the Crisis Points That Challenge Every Company and Career.* New York: Doubleday.

15 Crews, D. J., and D. M. Landers (1987), "A meta-analytic review of aerobic fitness and reactivity to psychosocial stressors." *Medicine and Science in Sport and Exercise* 19, 114–120.

16 Hobfall, Steven, and Alan Vaux (1993), "Social support: Social resources and social context," in Goldberger, Leo, and Shlomo Breznitz (eds.), *Handbook of Stress*. New York: Free Press, 695–697.

17 Benson, Herbert, M.D., with Marg Stark (1996), *Timeless Healing: The Power and Biology of Belief.* New York: Scribner, 17.

18 Justice, Blair (1987), *Who Gets Sick: How Beliefs, Moods, and Thoughts Affect Your Health.* Los Angeles: Jeremy Tarcher, 142–151.

Chapter 13

1 Davis, Stan, and Jim Botkin (1994), *The Monster under the Bed: How Business Is Mastering the Opportunity of Knowledge for Profit.* New York: Simon & Schuster, 49.

2 McGuire, James, and Phillip Priestley (1985), *Offending Behavior: Skills and Stratagems for Going Straight.* New York: St. Martin's Press.

   Romig, Dennis A. (1982), *Justice for Our Children.* Austin: Performance Research Press.

3 Pelz, Donald, and Frank Andrews (1966), *Scientists in Organizations: Productive Climates for Research and Development.* New York: John Wiley & Sons.

4 Case, John (1995), *Open-Book Management: The Coming Business Revolution.* New York: Harper Business.

5 Leonard (1995).

6 Sveiby, Karl (1997), *The New Organizational Wealth: Managing and Measuring Knowledge-Based Assets.* San Francisco: Berrett-Koehler, 23.

Chapter 14

1 Bennis, Warren, and Burt Nanus (1985), *Leaders: The Strategies for Taking Charge.* New York: Perennial Library.

2   Bass, Bernard (1981), *Handbook of Leadership: Theory, Research and Managerial Applications* (3rd ed.). New York: Free Press.

3   Lefton, Robert E., and V. R. Buzzota (1988), "Teams and teamwork: A study of executive-level teams." *National Productivity Review* (Winter 1987–88), 7–19.

4   Lefton and Buzzota (1988), 18.

5   Kelly, Robert E. (1998), *How to Be a Star at Work: Nine Breakthrough Strategies You Need to Succeed.* New York: Time Business.

6   Bass (1985), 42.

Hogan et al. (June 1994).

Kudisch, Jeffrey D., Mark L. Poteet, Gregory H. Dobbings, and Michael C. Rush (1995), "Expert power, referent power, and charisma: Toward the resolution of a theoretical debate." *Journal of Business & Psychology* 10, 177–195.

7   George, Jennifer M., and Kenneth Bettenhausen (1990), "Understanding prosocial behavior, sales performance and turnover: A group-level analysis in a service context." *Journal of Applied Psychology* 75(6), 698–709.

8   Seligman (1990).

9   Richardson, Robert J., and Katharine S. Thayer (1993), *The Charismatic Factor: How to Develop Your Natural Leadership Ability.* Englewood Cliffs, N.J.: Prentice-Hall, 33.

10   Kotter, J. P. (1982), *The General Managers.* New York: Free Press.

Kaplan, R. E. (1984), "Trade routes: The manager's network of relationships." *Organizational Dynamics* (Spring 1984), 37–52.

11   Chao, Georgia T., Pat M. Walz, and Philip D. Gardner (1992), "Formal and informal mentorships: A comparison on mentoring functions and contrast with nonmentored counterparts." *Personnel Psychology, A Journal of Applied Research* 45(3) (Autumn 1992), 619–636.

12   Clawson, J. G. (1980), "Mentoring in managerial careers," in Derr, C. B. (ed.), *Work, Family, and Career.* New York: Praeger.

13 Tushman, Michael, and David Nadler (1980), "Communication and technical roles in R&D laboratories: An information processing approach." *TIMS Studies in the Management Sciences* 15, 91–112.

Pelz and Andrews (1966).

Leonard (1995).

Chapter 15

1 Locke and Latham (1984).

2 Romig (2001).

3 Moses, Timothy P., and Anthony J. Stahelski (1999), "Productivity evaluation of teamwork at an aluminum manufacturing plant." *Group & Organization Management* 24(3), 391–412.

Hirokawa, Randy Y., and Kathryn M. Rost (1992), "Effective group decision making in organizations: Field test of the vigilant interaction theory." *Management Communication Quarterly* 5(3), 267–288.

Romig (1996).

4 Eisenhardt, K. M. (1989), "Making fast strategic decisions in high-velocity environments." *Academy of Management Journal* 32(3), 543–576.

5 Koch, J. L. (1979), "Effects of goal specificity and performance feedback to work groups on peer leadership, performance and attitudes." *Human Relations* 32(10), 819–840.

6 Pritchard et al. (1988).

7 Graen, George, Michael A. Novak, and Patricia Sommerkamp (1972), "The effects of leader-member exchange and job design on productivity and satisfaction: Testing a dual attachment model." *Organization Behavior and Human Performance* 30, 109–131.

Chapter 16

1 Collins, James C., and Jerry I. Porras (1994), *Built to Last: Successful Habits of Visionary Companies.* New York: Harper Business.

2 Kotter, John P., and James L. Heskett (1992), *Corporate Culture and Performance*. New York: Free Press.

3 Maloney, Dennis, Dennis Romig, and Troy Armstrong (1988), "Juvenile probation: The balanced approach." *Juvenile and Family Court Journal* 39, 1–63.

4 Hamel, Gary, and C. K. Prahalad (1989), "Strategic intent." *Harvard Business Review* 3 (May–June 1989), 67.

5 Wood et al. (1987).

6 Baghai, Mehrdad, Stephen Coley, and David White (1996), "Staircase to growth." *The McKinsey Quarterly* 4, 38–61.

7 Mintzberg, Henry (1994), *The Rise and Fall of Strategic Planning*. New York: Free Press.

8 Amoco Production Company (1989), *Organizational Communication Study*. Houston: Amoco Production Company.

9 Piaget, J. (1967), *Six Psychological Studies*. New York: Random House.

Lewin, Kurt (1950), "Group decision and social change," in Newcomb, T., & E. Hartley (eds.), *Readings in Social Psychology* (revised ed.). New York: Holt, Rinehart, & Winston.

Chapter 18

1 Conger, Jay, and Beth Benjamin (1999), *Building Leaders: How Successful Companies Develop the Next Generation*. San Francisco: Jossey-Bass, 52–53.

National Research Council (1991), *In the Mind's Eye: Enhancing Human Performance*. Washington, D.C: National Academy Press.

Recommended Reading

Personal Leadership

Benson, Herbert, M.D., with Marg Stark (1996), *Timeless Healing: The Power and Biology of Belief.* New York: Scribner.

Cooper, Kenneth H., M.D. (1977), *The Aerobics Way.* New York: Bantam Books.

Covey, Stephen R. (1994), *First Things First: To Live, to Love, to Learn, to Leave a Legacy.* New York: Simon & Schuster.

Covey, Stephen R. (1989), *The 7 Habits of Highly Effective People: Restoring the Character Ethic.* New York: Simon & Schuster.

Csikszentmihalyi, Mihaly (1997), *Finding Flow: The Psychology of Engagement with Everyday Life.* New York: Basic Books.

De Bono, Edward (1970), *Lateral Thinking: Creativity Step by Step.* New York: Harper Colophon Books.

Frankl, Victor E. (1959), *Man's Search for Meaning: An Introduction to Logotherapy.* New York: Washington Square Press.

Hendricks, Gay, and Kate Ludeman (1996), *The Corporate Mystic: A Guidebook for Visionaries with Their Feet on the Ground.* New York: Bantam Books.

Klitgaard, Robert, Ronald Maclean-Abaroa, and H. Lindsey Parris (2000), *Corrupt Cities: A Practical Guide to Cure and Prevention.* Oakland, Calif.: ICS Press.

Maddi, Salvatore R., and Suzanne C. Kobasa (1984), *The Hardy Executive: Health under Stress.* Homewood, Ill.: Dow Jones–Irwin.

Seligman, Martin E. P. (1990), *Learned Optimism: How to Change Your Mind and Your Life.* New York: Pocket Books.

Knowledge Leadership

Conot, Robert (1979), *A Streak of Luck: The Outrageous and Passionate Life of Thomas Alva Edison, Maverick Genius Who Captivated the World.* New York: Bantam Books.

Druckman, Daniel, and Robert A. Bjork, eds. (1991), *In the Mind's Eye: Enhancing Human Performance.* Washington, D.C.: National Academy Press.

Leonard, Dorothy (1998), *Wellsprings of Knowledge: Building and Sustaining the Sources of Innovation.* Boston: Harvard Business School Press.

Pfeffer, Jeffrey, and Robert I. Sutton (2000), *The Knowing-Doing Gap: How Smart Companies Turn Knowledge into Action.* Boston: Harvard Business School Press.

Rodin, Robert, with Curtis Hartman (1999), *Free, Perfect, and Now: Connecting to the Three Insatiable Customer Demands: A CEO's True Story.* New York: Simon & Schuster.

Rogers, Everett M. (1995), *Diffusion of Innovation.* New York: Free Press.

Sveiby, Karl Erik (1997), *The New Organizational Wealth: Managing & Measuring Knowledge-Based Assets.* San Francisco: Berrett-Koehler.

Interpersonal Leadership

Beebe, Steven A., and Susan J. Beebe (2000), *Public Speaking: An Audience-Centered Approach.* Needham Heights, Mass.: Allyn & Bacon.

Beebe, Steven A., Susan J. Beebe, and Diana K. Ivy (2001), *Communication: Principles for a Lifetime.* Needham Heights, Mass.: Allyn & Bacon.

Goleman, Daniel (1995), *Emotional Intelligence.* New York: Bantam Books.

Goleman, Daniel (1998), *Working with Emotional Intelligence.* New York: Bantam Books.

Kelly, Robert E. (1998), *How to Be a Star at Work: Nine Breakthrough Strategies You Need to Succeed.* New York: Times Books.

Misner, Ivan R., and Don Morgan (2000), *Masters of Networking: Building Relationships for Your Pocketbook and Soul.* Austin: Bard Press.

Team Leadership

Katzenbach, Jon R., and Douglas K. Smith (1993), *The Wisdom of Teams: Creating the High-Performance Organization.* Boston: Harvard Business School Press.

Larson, Carl E., and Frank M. J. LaFasto (1989), *Teamwork: What Must Go Right/What Can Go Wrong.* Newbury Park, Calif.: Sage.

Locke, Edwin A., and Gary P. Latham (1984), *Goal Setting: A Motivational Technique That Works!* Englewood Cliffs, N.J.: Prentice-Hall.

McLagan, Patricia, and Christo Nel (1995), *The Age of Participation: New Governance for the Workplace and the World.* San Francisco: Berrett-Koehler.

Orsburn, Jack D., Linda Moran, Ed Musselwhite, and John H. Zenger (2000), *The New Self-Directed Work Teams: Mastering the Challenge.* New York: McGraw-Hill.

Romig, Dennis A. (1996), *Breakthrough Teamwork: Outstanding Results Using Structured Teamwork.* Austin: Performance Research Press.

Organizational Leadership

Baghai, Mehrdad, Steven Coley, and David White (1999), *The Alchemy of Growth: Practical Insights for Building the Enduring Enterprise.* Reading, Mass.: Perseus Books.

Bass, Bernard M. (1985), *Leadership and Performance beyond Expectations.* New York: Free Press.

Bennis, Warren, and Burt Nanus (1985), *Leaders: The Strategies for Taking Charge.* New York: Harper & Row.

Collins, James C., and Jerry I. Porras (1994), *Built to Last: Successful Habits of Visionary Companies.* New York: Harper Business.

Conger, Jay A., and Beth Benjamin (1999), *Building Leaders: How Successful Companies Develop the Next Generation.* San Francisco: Jossey-Bass.

Davis, Stan, and Christopher Meyer (1998), *Blur: The Speed of Change in the Connected Economy.* Reading, Mass.: Addison-Wesley.

Kotter, John P., and James L. Heskett (1992), *Corporate Culture and Performance.* New York: Free Press.

Lowe, Janet (1998), *Jack Welch Speaks: Wisdom from the World's Greatest Business Leader.* New York: John Wiley & Sons.

Mintzberg, Henry (1994), *The Rise and Fall of Strategic Planning: Reconceiving Roles for Planning, Plans, Planners*. New York: Free Press.

Peters, Thomas J., and Robert H. Waterman Jr. (1982), *In Search of Excellence: Lessons from America's Best-Run Companies*. New York: Harper & Row.

Senge, Peter M. (1990), *The Fifth Discipline: The Art and Practice of the Learning Organization*. New York: Doubleday Currency.

Slater, Robert (1999), *Jack Welch and the GE Way*. New York: McGraw-Hill.

Spitzer, Dean R. (1995), *SuperMotivation: A Blueprint for Energizing Your Organization from Top to Bottom*. New York: Amacom.

Science of Side by Side

Axelrod, Robert, and Michael D. Cohen (1999), *Harnessing Complexity: Organizational Implications of a Scientific Frontier*. New York: Free Press.

Clippinger, John Henry III, ed. (1999), *The Biology of Business: Decoding the Natural Laws of Enterprise*. San Francisco: Jossey-Bass.

Damasio, Antonio (1999), *The Feeling of What Happens: Body and Emotion in the Making of Consciousness*. New York: Harcourt Brace.

De Waal, Frans (1996), *Good Natured: The Origins of Right and Wrong in Humans and Other Animals*. Cambridge, Mass.: Harvard University Press.

De Waal, Frans (1989), *Peacemaking among Primates*. Cambridge, Mass.: Harvard University Press.

Dugatkin, Lee Alan (1997), *Cooperation among Animals: An Evolutionary Perspective*. New York: Oxford University Press.

Hazlitt, Henry (1946), *Economics in One Lesson*. New York: Manor Books.

Howard, Pierce J. (2000), *The Owner's Manual for the Brain* (2nd ed.). Austin: Bard Press.

Kerr, Michael E., and Murray Bowen (1988), *Family Evaluation: An Approach Based on Bowen Theory.* New York: W. W. Norton.

LeDoux, Joseph (1996), *The Emotional Brain: The Mysterious Underpinnings of Emotional Life.* New York: Touchstone.

Papero, Daniel V. (1990), *Bowen Family Systems Theory.* Needham Heights, Mass.: Allyn & Bacon.

Sapolsky, Robert M. (1994), *Why Zebras Don't Get Ulcers: A Guide to Stress, Stress-Related Diseases, and Coping.* New York: W. H. Freeman.

Sulloway, Frank J. (1996), *Born to Rebel: Birth Order, Family Dynamics, and Creative Lives.* New York: Vintage Books.

Wheatley, Margaret J. (1992), *Leadership and the New Science.* San Francisco: Berrett-Koehler.

Index

S

About the Author

You may feel frustrated with the lack of progress and performance where you work. You may even need a miracle. Dr. Romig's colleagues joke about his ability to bring about miraculous results in training leaders. Dennis says it's simple: just use leadership practices based on scientific research.

Science has produced miracles in medicine, communication, and transportation. Dennis is creating a science of leadership that can achieve miracles for businesses, governments, and charitable organizations. He collects hard-data research studies the way some people collect baseball cards.

Dennis received his Ph.D. in educational psychology and management from the University of Texas. He spent hundreds of hours being trained in statistics and research methods. Previously he obtained a master's degree in counseling psychology and a bachelors' degree in basic science (chemistry and biology). He achieved all three degrees in six years.

Dennis is president of Performance Resources, Inc., an international training and consulting firm headquartered in Austin. He provides leadership training and coaching to CEOs and other executives at their companies or at the Side by Side Leadership Academy in Austin. He leads a group of highly successful trainers and consultants who facilitate outstanding results throughout the world.

An award-winning author, Dennis won the best paper award at the International Work Teams Conference in 1995. His previous book, *Breakthrough Teamwork,* received the highest rating at Amazon.com. Dennis serves on several boards, including the board of directors of MetroNational Corporation in Houston.

About PRI

Dennis Romig is the president of Performance Resources, Inc. (PRI), an international "think and do tank" headquartered in Austin, Texas. Dennis and the PRI trainers and consultants have trained over 10,000 leaders. PRI's training programs and materials help leaders obtain results sometimes beyond their wildest imagination.

A wide range of benefits are reported by PRI clients:

- Corporations gain up to 300 percent improvement in shareholder value.

- Organizations achieve significant increases in worker productivity.

- Motivated workers volunteer to complete actions to achieve goals or solve problems.

- Team and leadership skills are applied not only inside the organization but outside, with customers, partners, and suppliers.

- The creativity and innovation of everyone is increased.

These clients have achieved outstanding results:

Business and Industry

- Advanced Micro Devices, Inc. (AMD)
- Amoco
- Asea Brown Boveri (ABB)
- Beckman Coulter
- Burlington Resources

- Corning
- Dell Computer Corporation
- E-Systems
- Falconer Glass Industries
- Johnson & Johnson
- MetroNational Corporation
- Monsanto
- Moog Aircraft Group
- Motorola
- Noble Affiliates
- Raytheon
- International SEMATECH
- ST Microelectronics
- Texas Instruments
- Westinghouse

Government, Nonprofit, and Religious Organizations

- City of Austin
- Community of Christ World Church
- Oregon Juvenile Justice Alliance
- Sisters of Charity
- State of Texas Health and Human Services Coordinating Council
- Texas Senate
- United States Department of Justice
- University of Indiana
- Washington State Department of Social and Health Services

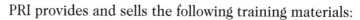

PRI provides and sells the following training materials:

Leadership

- Side by Side Leadership Handbook
- Side by Side Team Leadership Handbook
- Side by Side Organizational Leadership Handbook
- Sponsoring Side by Side Breakthrough Teams
- Side by Side Coaching
- Organizational Breakthrough Assessment

Teamwork

- Side by Side Teamwork Guide for Line Workers
- Side by Side Teamwork Guide for Knowledge Workers
- Side by Side Teamwork International Version
- Side by Side Teamwork Facilitator Guide for Line Workers
- Side by Side Teamwork Facilitator Guide for Knowledge Workers
- Team Conflict Management Handbook
- Side by Side Team Assessment Kit
- Side by Side Teamwork Start-up Handbook

PRI Programs

- Side by Side Leadership Academy: Austin (three days)
- Team Leadership Skills (two days)
- Organizational Leadership Skills (two days)
- Side by Side Leadership Workshop (various cities)
- Side by Side Client Workshop (customized for specific business results)

Contact Performance Resources, Inc. at sidebyside.com or at 800-204-3118.

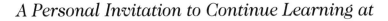

A Personal Invitation to Continue Learning at

www.sidebyside.com

I hope and fully expect that you will achieve great success when you try out the ideas in this book. As you learn and apply the principles of Side by Side Leadership, you may wish to keep up with the latest developments in this field. For this reason, my colleagues and I invite you to visit our web site, www.sidebyside.com. We will be using this resource to provide

- Tips for how to learn and apply the twenty skills of Side by Side Leadership

- Newly identified Side by Side skills

- Ways to develop your own skills and tools

- Experiences of successful leaders

- Case studies of organizational success

One reason leaders get the outstanding results reported in this book is that the Side by Side model and leadership practices are based upon the best research studies from both the behavioral and natural sciences. The multidisciplinary field of natural systems thinking continues to conduct research, analyze new findings, and formulate new theories and principles. Our web site will report the latest research and conclusions to show how leaders can facilitate improved productivity.

Among other benefits, sidebyside.com will give you access to the latest developed assessments and evaluation tools. There will be an area for sharing your successes and asking questions, and we will use other interactive learning methods. We invite you to become an active part of this rapidly developing field of knowledge.

Acknowledgments and Thanks

The Side by Side Leadership model was developed by finding and summarizing hard-data research and then applying Side by Side principles to improve performance in business. Hillary Keith, Bo Shapiro, and my two daughters-in-law, Lisa and Nadine Romig, were especially helpful in mining for the gold nuggets of research. Along the way of creating a scientific model for leadership, I found the Bowen Center in Washington, D.C. Before his death, Murray Bowen, the founder, worked to bridge psychology and the behavioral sciences with biology and the natural sciences. I want to thank my teachers, now colleagues, who are continuing to develop and apply Bowen's Natural Systems Theory to help families, organizations, and communities: Hal DeShong, Victoria Harrison, Michael Kerr, Dan Papero, and others.

After behavioral sciences and natural systems theory were synthesized, Terry Ross, Bob Watt, Matt Rollins, Mike Bown, Steve Beebe, and Paul Radde helped me think through what mutual leadership really means and how it can improve productivity.

I am grateful to the leaders who have used Side by Side Leadership to improve their organization's performance. They have showed me how spectacular the results of being a Side by Side leader can be: Gary Heerssen, Jim Doran, Preston Snuggs, Mike Greig, Chuck Davidson, Mike Wiley, Chip Gill, T. Don Stacy, John Van Brunt, Roy Johnson, Grant McMurray, Ken Robinson, Dave Williams, Frank Campbell, Sheri Brainard, John Smith, Dennis Maloney, and many others.

All of the above people and I knew that Side by Side Leadership worked. The challenge was how to write it in a book. Keith McGowan, Ellen Sheldon, Jeff Morris, and Ray Bard of Bard Press came to the rescue. Jeff and Ray helped put in book form the relaxed, Side by Side way that my colleagues and I train, coach, and consult with leaders. Jeff and Ray are the best. They, along with the following reviewers, share the credit for the readability of the book: Leslie Baker, Nancy Bartlett, Keith Bonham, Les Bowd, Eric Cox, Charles Davenport, Jack Flannery, Pam Holloway, Bob Keenan, Chris Keith, Barbara Kreisman, Andy Levine, Michael Lovas, Gary McDonald, Bev Powell, Bronwyn Richards, Keith Romig, Mike Romig, Ron Romig, Tom Swails, Darryl Townsend, Mike Webb, and Cynthia Wilder.

Laurie Romig took over as president of Performance Resources, Inc. to allow me to write *Side by Side Leadership,* and provided encouragement every step of the way. Thanks, Laurie.

Dennis A. Romig

Notes

Notes